CAVALRY UNIFORMS

INCLUDING OTHER MOUNTED TROOPS
OF BRITAIN AND THE COMMONWEALTH

CAVALRY UNIFORMS

INCLUDING OTHER MOUNTED TROOPS
OF BRITAIN AND THE COMMONWEALTH
in colour

by

ROBERT and CHRISTOPHER
WILKINSON-LATHAM

Illustrated by
JACK CASSIN-SCOTT

The Notes on Swords and Weapons specially written
for this volume by Major John Wilkinson-Latham

BLANDFORD PRESS
LONDON

SBN 7137 0134 X

Colour printed in Great Britain by Colour Reproductions Ltd.,
Billericay. Text set in Monotype Times New Roman, printed and bound in
Great Britain by Richard Clay (The Chaucer Press), Ltd., Bungay, Suffolk

PREFACE

This is the first book of its kind to be devoted entirely to the uniforms and weapons of mounted troops of the British and Commonwealth Armies, and to have 96 pages in colour.

While compiling this work we have taken care to examine wherever possible the actual items depicted. If this has not been possible the pictorial evidence, supported by contemporary written evidence, has been selected. In this volume we have presented both the typical and the unusual to give an overall picture of mounted troops from 1742 until the present day.

Great care has been taken with the illustrations, and close-ups of weapons and equipment have been shown to add more detail to the text. Seventy-six British regiments have been shown and 20 Commonwealth regiments.

We hope that this volume will fill the need for a ready source of information for both the beginner and the advanced student of military uniforms and equipment, and as a reference book for the model-soldier enthusiast.

We wish to thank the following in the writing of this book for either providing information or allowing us to examine items in their collections:

Mr. W. Y. Carman of the National Army Museum
A. Caton of Norman Newton (Tradition) Ltd.
Mr. J. Fabb of A. & R. Fabb Bros.
Major G. J. Flint-Shipman
Capt. Hollies Smith of Parker Galleries
Mr. B. Mollo of the National Army Museum
Mr. J. Rowntree
H.M. Tower of London
National Army Museum
Wilkinson Sword Limited (uniform pattern book)

Our thanks to Mrs. M. H. Craven for patiently typing and retyping the manuscript and for deciphering our unreadable writing.

Lastly, but by no means least, to our mother, a source of unflagging confidence when the work seemed never-ending.

ROBERT WILKINSON-LATHAM
CHRISTOPHER WILKINSON-LATHAM

42 Berkeley Street,
London W.1

INTRODUCTION

The study of British military uniforms is a hobby that now has more adherents than ever, probably brought about by the drabness of modern combat uniform, which stems from the tremendously changed character of twentieth-century warfare.

At a previous time in history uniforms were also dull and uninteresting, and nothing was less exciting, possibly, than the uniforms worn by Cromwell's Ironsides. However, between 1660 and the present day uniforms rose to a gorgeous and extravagant crescendo, which was at its height in the first half of the nineteenth century and probably reached its peak with Bingham's Dandies (17th Light Dragoons), Cardigan's Cherrybums (the 11th Hussars) and the exotic uniforms of India.

An old uniform jacket lying in an old oak chest may not by itself stir anyone's imagination with past glories; but if it can be identified with its regiment and period, and this knowledge linked with the glorious history of Britain and her Empire, then we can start building around this relic of long ago a fascinating story which will bring back to life some past deed of heroism or some hitherto unknown chapter of men who gave their lives in the cause of freedom.

The psychology of colours is in itself a subject which is beyond the scope of this small book, but modern psychologists have paid great attention to the effect that colours have in everyday life. The colour red, by itself, has always had a connotation of danger and also has the effect of stirring the blood, hence the expression 'seeing red' as a synonym for anger. One sees also the use of this colour in the bull ring, where the matador's cloak has always been bright scarlet. The Thin Red Line of the 93rd, the Argyle & Sutherland Highlanders in the Crimea, and the splendid tunic of the 16th, the Scarlet Lancers, have done much to deter the enemy.

Blue in army uniforms has always indicated a personal link with the Sovereign, and its use as a facing colour has been confined to Royal regiments. On the other hand, black has seldom been used in the British Army: it is a sinister colour, reminiscent of the hangman, and its use by the S.S. and the Death's Head Hussars in the German Armies is within living memory.

At one time soldiering was the hobby of the sons and heirs of some of the most noble and richest families in the land, and in those days, when commissions and even the command of regiments could be purchased, competition was great in the field of outfitting your regiment so that its uniforms and accoutrements outstripped in beauty those of its contemporaries.

Regimental nicknames often stemmed from the glory or colours of the uniform: the Life Guards are known universally throughout the Army as the Tins, because of their cuirasses, and the Horse Guards have been known as the Blues for nearly 300 years from the blue uniform with which they were outfitted by the Earl of Oxford. The 2nd Dragoon Guards, the Queen's Bays, were always known as the Bays from 1767, when they were the only Cavalry regiment to be mounted exclusively on bay horses. The Old Canaries, the 3rd Prince of Wales' Dragoon Guards, took their name from the canary-yellow facings on their uniforms, and the 5th Royal Inniskilling Dragoon Guards were nicknamed the Green Horse from their regimental colour adopted in Ireland. The 2nd Dragoons, Royal Scots Greys, were another regiment where the exclusive use of a particular coloured horse gave the regiment its soubriquet The Greys, and the 5th Royal Irish Lancers became known as the Redbreasts from the scarlet facings and plastrons on their lancer tunics. The 6th Inniskilling Dragoons were known throughout the Army as the Black Dragoons, taken once again from the colour of their mounts; and the 7th Queen's Own Hussars, known as the Lilywhite 7th, wore white facings from 1690 to 1818. One other regiment which deserves special mention with its nickname is the Grey Lancers, the 21st Empress of India's, whose lancer tunic was resplendent with a French grey plastron. The lesser-known Cape Town Cavalry rejoiced in the nickname of the 'Sparklers'.

The regiments of Yeomanry Cavalry, which mostly commenced their history in the last decade of the eighteenth century as volunteers raised to defend the country against the expected invasion by the French, had always up until 1939 been resplendent in uniform and had always managed to add some little extra feature to the style of uniform of the Regular Cavalry regiments with which they were associated. One particular extra adornment was that of the scarlet breeches of an officer of the Westmorland & Cumberland Yeomanry, which had silver-embroidered Austrian knots on the front of the thighs. The Commonwealth Volunteer Units were also dressed in the same slightly elaborate style as their British counterparts.

There has been a profusion of different patterns of headgear, which has come about for various reasons. The bearskin cap of the Brigade of Guards stems originally from the desire of the King of Prussia to have the tallest personal guard in the world. The men he recruited for this were all over 6 ft 6 in. in height and, to make certain that they were not topped, he outfitted them with bearskin caps some 18 in. high, bringing the height of his guards to 8 ft tall. This must have had an awe-inspiring effect on any troops of lesser stature, and here it is worth remembering that the average height of men 100 years ago was nothing like it is today. Most of the antique uniforms that are found are of incredibly small sizes by modern-day standards.

The slim-waisted lancer cap derived from the *schapka* of the Polish Lancers, and was more decorative than useful. In fact, in the Crimea men were issued with the foul-weather lance cap cover in plain black. The hussar busby and the dragoon helmet had a purpose, in that they both afforded some protection to the head from sword-cuts, and in some earlier cases where dragoon helmets carried a large fur crest this also added to their defensive qualities.

When fighting broke out in South Africa in the latter few years of the last century the use of colour in military uniforms was shown to be a disadvantage, and khaki, which had been adopted in India at about the time of the Mutiny, was far more suited to the guerilla and commando types of warfare practised by the Boers.

Men in uniform never cease to be an attraction to the general public. The guard-mounting ceremonies at Buckingham Palace, Horse Guards and Windsor Castle attract an audience of many millions each year. The annual Royal Tournament in London is invariably a 'sell-out'. Whenever the King's Troop, Royal Horse Artillery, fire their salutes in Hyde Park, it is amazing how many people appear from seemingly nowhere to stand and watch. In Canada the resplendent sight of the Governor General's Body Guard on ceremonial escort duty has the same splendour as the Household Cavalry. The National Army Museum is a storehouse of knowledge for all those who are interested in the great history of the British Army, and there they have an incomparable collection of uniforms which will always be a treasured reminder of the days when wars were fought in splendour.

The ceremonial parade, whether in Britain, Canada, Australia or anywhere in the Commonwealth, still thrills the crowd that watches and is a reminder of the still strong bond between the Armed Forces of the United Kingdom and Commonwealth countries.

NOTE

The Plates and their relative descriptive material have been placed in date order and not in order of seniority. Where there coincides more than one regiment at any particular date, the following order of precedence has been adopted:

Royal Horse Artillery (always accorded the position of Right of the Line when parading with their guns).
Household Cavalry.
Heavy Cavalry.
Light Cavalry.
Yeomanry Cavalry.
Dominion and Commonwealth Cavalry.

1 **1st Troop Life Guards.** Trooper 1742

2 **Royal Horse Guards.** Trooper 1742

3 **2nd Horse Grenadiers.** Trooper 1750

4 **15th Light Dragoons.** Drummer 1750

5 **6th Dragoons**. Trooper 1751

6 **11th Dragoons.** Farrier 1758

7 **15th Light Dragoons.** Trooper 1759

8 **2nd Dragoon Guards.** Trooper 1760

9 **16th Light Dragoons.** Trooper 1776

10 **17th Light Dragoons.** Trooper 1790

11   **Royal Horse Artillery.** Officer 1793

12 **16th Light Dragoons**. Officer 1793

13 10th Light Dragoons. Trooper 1794

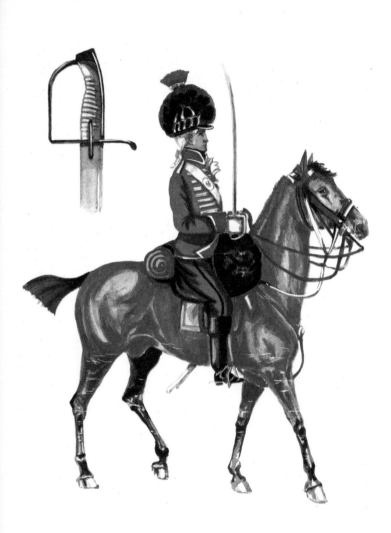

14 Shropshire Provisional Cavalry. Trooper 1794

15 **4th Dragoons.** Officer 1807

16   **7th Hussars**. Officer 1807

17 **6th Dragoon Guards.** Officer 1808

18 **6th Dragoons.** Officer 1810

19 **6th Dragoons**. Officer 1811

20 **10th Hussars**. Trooper 1812

21 **Royal Horse Guards.** Officer 1814

22   Royal Horse Artillery. Officer 1815

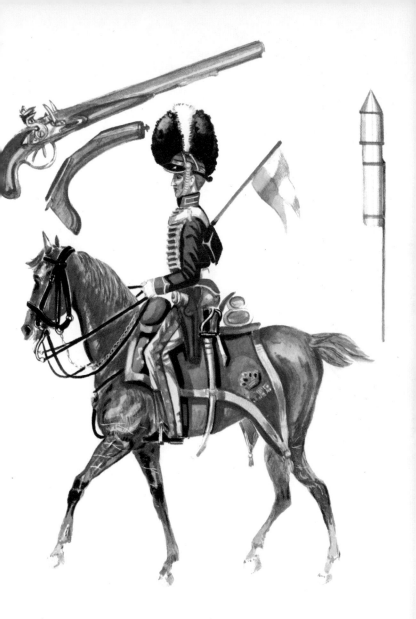

23 Royal Horse Artillery (Rocket Troop). Gunner 1815

24 **2nd Dragoons.** Officer 1815

25 **1st Life Guards.** Officer 1817

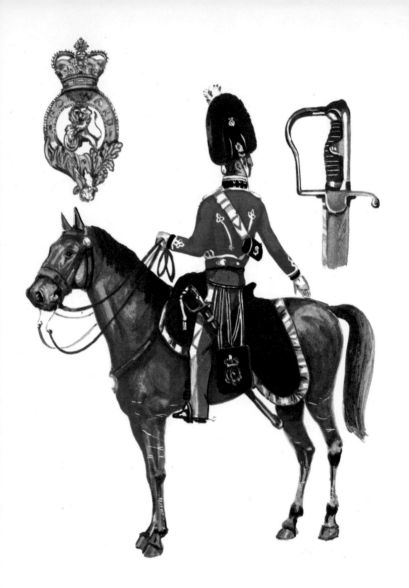

26 **Light Horse Volunteers.** Trooper 1817

27 **2nd Life Guards.** Officer 1820

28 4th Light Dragoons. Officer 1820

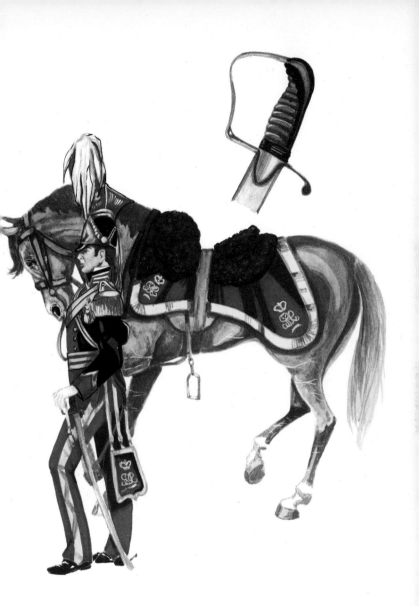

29 **9th Lancers.** Officer 1820

30 **6th Bengal Light Cavalry.** Officer 1825

31 **Royal Horse Artillery.** Officer 1828

32   **8th Hussars**. Officer 1828

33 **5th Dragoon Guards.** Officer 1831

34 **Worcestershire Yeomanry.** Officer 1832

35 **Aide-de-Camp to the King.** 1834

36 **Royal Horse Guards.** Officer 1834

37 **15th Hussars**. Officer 1834

38 **2nd Dragoon Guards.** Officer 1836

39 **South Salopian Yeomanry.** Officer 1842

40 **3rd Dragoon Guards.** Officer 1844

41   **3rd Light Dragoons.** Officer 1846

42 **1st Bengal Light Cavalry.** Officer 1846

43 **1st Dragoon Guards.** Officer 1847

44　**Gloucester Hussars.** Officer 1847

45 **Bundelekund Legion.** Officer 1847

46 **1st Madras Light Cavalry.** Officer 1848

47 **2nd Dragoons.** Sergeant 1854

48 **4th Light Dragoons.** Trooper 1854

49 **8th Hussars**. Trooper 1854

50 **11th Hussars.** Officer 1854

51 **13th Light Dragoons.** Trooper 1854

52 **17th Lancers.** Trooper 1854

53   **Royal Horse Artillery.** Officer 1855

54 **16th Lancers.** Trooper 1855

55 **4th Light Dragoons.** Officer 1856

56 **Prince Alfred's Own Cape Town Cavalry.** Officer 1860

57 **17th Lancers.** Officer 1865

58 Taplow Lancers. Officer 1870

59 **Canterbury Yeomanry Cavalry.** Trooper 1875

60 **1st Dragoon Guards.** Officer 1879

61   **11th Hussars.** Trooper 1881

62 **2nd Dragoons.** Sergeant 1882

63　**Camel Detachment.** Trooper 1884

64 **Royal Horse Guards.** Drummer 1887

65 **10th Hussars**. Officer 1888

66 **2nd Life Guards**. Farrier 1890

67 **Governor General's Body Guard (Canada).** Trooper 1890

68 **Shropshire Yeomanry.** Trooper 1892

69 **Gloucester Hussars.** Trooper 1896

70   **18th Hussars.** Trooper 1899

71 **Victoria Mounted Rifles.** Officer 1899

72   **New South Wales Lancers.** Trooper 1900

73 **6th Dragoon Guards.** Trooper 1901

74 **6th Dragoons.** Sergeant 1901

75 **16th Lancers.** Trooper 1901

76 **Imperial Yeomanry.** Trooper 1901

77 Bethune's Mounted Infantry. Officer 1901

78 **21st Lancers**. Trooper 1904

79   **Royal Artillery Mounted Band.** Drummer 1905

80   **King's Colonials.** Officer 1908

81 **25th Cavalry.** Camel Sowar 1908

82 **Glamorgan Yeomanry.** Officer 1909

83 **Skinner's Horse.** Sowar 1909

84   **14th (Murray's Jats) Lancers**. Risaldar Major 1909

85   **29th Deccan Horse**. Risaldar 1910

86 **City of London Yeomanry (Rough Riders).** Officer 1912

87 **Oxford Hussars.** Officer 1914

88 **5th Lancers**. Trooper 1918

89   **British South Africa Police.** Trooper 1924

90 **1st Dragoon Guards.** Trumpeter 1927

91 **Somaliland Camel Corps.** Sergeant 1932

92　**Ayrshire Yeomanry.** Officer 1936

93 **Governor General's Body Guard.** Trumpeter 1938

94 **13th (Duke of Cornwall's Own) Lancers.** Drummer 1938

95　**Transjordan Frontier Force.** Sergeant 1938

96 **Life Guards.** Trooper 1953

1. 1st Troop Life Guards.
Trooper, 1742

Head Dress

The head dress worn by the Life Guards, and in fact by most soldiers of the Army except Grenadiers, was the tricorne hat as described in the Clothing Warrant of 1742. It was a broad-brimmed black felt hat turned up on both sides and at the back. The brim of the hat in the case of the Life Guards was edged in a band of gold lace. On the left-hand side was a black silk rosette with a gold lace loop and regimental pattern button in the centre

Uniform

A long scarlet coat without any lapels was worn, and with pairs of gold lace loops on either side of the front of the coat, with buttons at the extremities, of regimental pattern. The coat was lined in blue and buttoned back to reveal this colour at the side. Below the white stock worn at the neck was a piece of blue material edged with gold and buttoned to both sides of the small gold-edged red collar. The cuffs had a large distinct flap with lace loops and regimental-pattern button, the whole of the slash being edged in gold. The cuffs had gold lace loops underneath the slashed flap, about 6 in number. The pocket flaps on either hip were parted in the centre edged with gold lace and had 4 button loops. Below the flap were 4 buttons. The waistcoat was buff and single-breasted, as were the breeches, worn buttoned at the knee. Black boots with extra protection at

the front but low at the back were worn with spurs. White linen knee protectors were worn and appeared above the level of the top of the boot. The gauntlets were of buff leather, and the cloaks were red lined with blue.

Accoutrements

The carbine belt was of gold lace, backed with leather, with 2 bands of the troop colours, in this case red. The belt held a carbine swivel on the right hip. The sword-belt was also of gold with 2 bands of red 1st Troop lace, and the sword was slung in a baldrick on the left hip. The buckle was a large, gilt brass one. The saddle cloth was red, edged in 2 bands of gold lace with a red band in the centre and with the Royal cipher in a Garter surmounted by a crown. The holster covers were of the same design (shown in detail in close-up).

Note: Powdered pigtails were worn by troopers in the Household Cavalry and not by other soldiers, but as they were classed as gentlemen troopers, they wore their hair like the officers.

Weapons

Sword. The sword had a heavy brass bowl guard with a brass ball pommel. There was no backpiece, and the spirally cut wooden grip was bound with black leather. The blade was straight, 35 in. long, and carried in a black leather scabbard with top and bottom mounts, the top mount being equipped with a stud for frog suspension.

Carbine. They also carried a flintlock

carbine of 17 bore, patterned on the Brown Bess musket, stocked in walnut with brass furniture. Examples of these weapons are extremely rare, and they appear to have had a 27-in. barrel. It seems that they were made only in small quantities.

2. Royal Horse Guards.
Trooper, 1742

Head Dress

The head dress worn by the Royal Horse Guards in 1742 was that as described in the Clothing Warrant of 1742. It was a black felt hat with a wide brim looped up on all 3 sides forming the tricorne hat. The edges were bound in yellow lace, and on the left side was a black silk rosette with a regimental-pattern button in the centre.

Uniform

The coat was in blue material, extending to below the knees and worn with the skirts turned back and buttoned, revealing the red lining. The coat had no collar and was worn open, revealing a red waistcoat beneath. It had a single row of brass buttons down the front. A blue epaulette held with a small button kept the crossbelt in place. The breeches were blue with white knee covers, and high black boots with reinforced tops were worn. The cuffs of the coat were red, with buttons, and buttons were also on the sleeve. Buff gloves were worn. A white stock was worn.

Accoutrements

A buff, leather-covered crossbelt with large pouch was worn over the left shoulder with, in the centre of the belt, a red flask cord holding a powder flask. Over the right shoulder a buff, leather crossbelt with large sword baldrick was worn, the baldrick and pouch hanging on the respective hips. The housings and holster covers were red with embroidered Royal arms and supporters in full colour. The edges of both the housings and holster covers had embroidered borders of scrolls, leaves and so on, in white.

Weapons

Sword. In the middle of the eighteenth century Heavy Cavalry carried a basket-hilted back sword with a long straight blade, terminating in a spear point, the hilt being very much akin to the Venetian schiavona and the Scottish basket-hilt. Depending upon the regiment, these were in either steel or brass and, though giving full protection to the hand, tended to cramp and restrict the exercises that could be performed with the sword.

Scabbards were mostly of leather, with a metal top-mount and chape, the top-mount bearing a stud so that the sword could be carried slung across the shoulder in a baldrick.

There were many variations of hilt piercing, depending upon the regiment and the particular whim of the commanding officer.

Pistol. In addition to the sword noted above, troopers carried the land service pistol. This was a weapon with a 12-in. barrel of 17 or carbine bore, the bulbous butt having a long-eared brass cap, brass trigger guard and ramrod pipe; the furniture being of walnut. The lock was the standard flint carbine lock, the entire weapon being some 18–20 in. in length.

3. 2nd (or Scots Troop) Horse Grenadiers. Trooper, 1750

Head Dress

The 'mitre' cap, as it was called, was worn by all mounted Grenadiers and all infantry Grenadiers. The 2nd (or Scots Troop) Grenadiers' 'mitre' cap had a red cloth front 12 in. high, edged in white lace. In the centre of this was the Royal cipher G.R. in yellow worsted embroidery on a red ground, encircled by the Garter and motto *Honi soit qui mal y pense*. A crown in heraldic colours surmounted this. On each side of the front and the Garter was an embroidered pattern in white of roses, thistles and foliage. The front flap was blue edged on the top in yellow lace, with motto *Nemo me impune lacersit*. Underneath this was a large, white embroidered thistle with leaves and a scroll and motto. The headband at the back, also in blue cloth, had embroidered crossed swords and carbines. Above the headband there was a blue bag falling at the top, sometimes worn stiffened, with a worsted tassel at the top.

Uniform

A scarlet coat without lapels was worn; there were large cuffs with 3 buttons, the buttonholes being dec-orated with white tape of regimental pattern. The coat was long to just above the knees, and buttoned back to reveal a blue lining. Five 'V's of white tape of regimental pattern ornamented each skirt of the coat. In the centre of each 'V' was a button. The lace had a blue line in it. Across the back was a 'V' of lace above the long vent. The front of the coat was worn buttoned at the top and sloping away. The buttonholes were of regimental pattern white tape. The left epaulette was red cloth and the right epaulette was white cord looped on the end of the shoulder, hanging down in loops to above the elbow. The low collar was red. The waistcoat and breeches were buff-coloured. Around the neck a white stock was worn. The breeches buttoned on the outside. Large black boots, rising above the knee at the front with a drop at the back to enable the wearer to bend his knee, completed the uniform. Large steel spurs were worn.

Accoutrements

A white buff crossbelt with brass buckle was worn over the left shoulder. A large leather ammunition box was worn. A swivel on the belt held the carbine. A red flask cord ran down the centre of the belt, terminating in a small priming flash worn on the right hip over the ammunition box. A white buff waist-belt was worn with brass buckle, to which a sword frog was attached on the left hip. The saddle cloth or housing was in two parts, and was red with Garter and cipher. The rear part was rounded and edged in yellow lace with

115

blue centre stripe. The holster covers were red with crown above Garter and cipher and were also surrounded with yellow lace with blue centre line.

Weapons

Carbine. The carbine carried at this period was developed from the standard weapon of the infantry of the period, i.e. the Brown Bess. The bore of this carbine was 17 balls to the pound, and it had an overall length of about 43 in. Examples of this weapon are rare, and it is not possible to say whether different manufacturers incorporated slightly different features. It was a flintlock weapon using in all cases the standard Brown Bess musket lock.

Sword. The sword was long, straight-bladed and with a heavy back and a single edge. The hilt was two brass bars with a bulbous brass pommel and the grip of leather. It was carried in a black leather scabbard with top and bottom mounts, the top mount bearing a stud for carriage in a baldrick.

4. 15th Light Dragoons. Drummer, 1750

Head Dress

The head dress of the drummers was, as in common with other regiments of Light Dragoons, a leather skull with comb and front plate. The plate was black japanned and edged in white metal with a crown surmounting a GR, these also in white metal. The turban was green, bound round the lower part of the helmet, knotting at the back, and falling down and ending in a tassel on each. The turban was bound to the helmet with white metal chain. Reinforcing bands were fitted on each side to give added protection from sabre cuts. The comb was white metal, ornamented on the sides and with a medusa head at the front. Into this was fitted a red horsehair plume.

Uniform

A green coat was worn, green being the regimental face colour until 1766, when it was changed to blue. It was the usual practice for bandsmen to wear coats with the colours, not as usual, but in reverse, i.e. green coat with scarlet facings. The coat had a scarlet collar, bound in white. The buttonholes were taped in white lace with a red band in the centre. The whole coat was decorated in white lace with red centre in 'V's on the arm and in 'V's at the waist, continued down straight to the bottom of the coat. The epaulettes were white with wing ends. The coat was lined white and turned back to reveal the white lining. A white waistcoat was worn. The breeches were white, buttoned above the knee, and with white knee protectors; black boots with reinforced tops and steel spurs completed the uniform. Ruffles were worn on the cuffs and on the stock.

Accoutrements

A crossbelt was worn, of white edged scarlet and with green centre. The waist-belt held a frog on the left hip from which was attached a bandsman's sword. The housing was green, edged in white with a red centre stripe. The letters XV LD appeared on the hindquarters, surrounded by a wreath of foliage. On the front housing was a crown over the Royal cipher GR. The drum carried on the left side was green with red hoops and roped in white. The design was a hound chasing a stag on a red background within a wreath of roses and thistles, below which was a scroll with the motto 'The swift, the vigilant and bold'.

Weapon

Sword. Cavalry bandsmen carried a sword designed by, or certainly approved by, their commanding officers. This was usually an extravagantly curved weapon and the hilt configuration usually a product of their commander's imagination. The usual habit was to have the pommel representing an animal of the chase, and the resulting weapons were peculiar to the regiments and their commanding officers at any particular time.

5. 6th Dragoons. Trooper, 1751

Head Dress

The head dress worn at this period was virtually identical for both Dragoons and Heavy Dragoons. It was of black felt-like material with a wide brim, laced up on all 3 sides to form the well-known tricorne hat. The edge of the hat was bound with

white lace in the case of the 6th Dragoons and had, on the left side, a black silk bow or rosette with a loop of white cord and a regimental-pattern button.

Uniform

The uniform worn by the other ranks of the 6th Dragoons was a long, red coat extending to the knee and worn with the front and back skirts turned back to reveal the lining, which was yellow. The coat was worn open to reveal beneath it the waistcoat and stock. The buttons on the uniform were grouped in threes and taped with regimental pattern lace. The cuffs were yellow with 2 groups of 3 'V's of lace, with the button in the centre of each 'V'. The yellow shoulder strap was worn on the left side of the coat, and on the right side a white cord aiguillette or shoulder knot hung down from the end of the shoulder. The breeches, which buttoned above the knee and below, were of buff leather; heavy, black dragoon boots with white stockings around the knee, and steel spurs, completed the uniform.

Accoutrements

A wide, buff crossbelt was worn over the left shoulder with a buff pouch containing carbine ammunition and certain personal items of necessity. The belt was fastened on the chest with a large brass buckle. A waistbelt with sword frog on the left hip was worn. The saddle housing and cloth were of yellow material edged in white with a blue centre line with a regimental device on the rear of each side. The holster covers were of the same colour, with the crown and Royal cipher. A carbine bucket was worn on the right side below the holster in which the butt of the carbine was inserted. It is interesting to note that the horses had their tails docked.

Weapons

Sword. In the middle of the eighteenth century Heavy Cavalry carried a basket-hilted back sword with a long straight blade, terminating in a spear point, the hilt being very much akin to the Venetian schiavona and the Scottish basket-hilt. Depending upon the regiment, these were in either steel or brass, and though giving full protection to the hand, tended to cramp and restrict the exercises that could be performed with the sword.

Scabbards were mostly of leather, with a metal top-mount and chape, the top-mount bearing a stud so that the sword could be carried slung across the shoulder in a baldrick. There were many variations of hilt piercing, depending upon the regiment and the particular whim of the commanding officer.

Pistol. In addition to the sword noted above, troopers carried the land service pistol. This was a weapon with a 12-in. barrel of 17 or carbine bore, the bulbous butt having a long-eared brass cap, brass trigger guard and ramrod pipe; the furniture being of walnut. The lock was the standard flint carbine lock, the entire weapon being some 18–20 in. in length.

6. 11th Dragoons. Farrier, 1758

Head Dress

The head dress was a bearskin cap of the infanty grenadier pattern. The cap was mitre-shaped at the front and at the back had a scarlet patch with white cords and tassels. The front plate in the case of farriers was of metal painted in red. In the centre was a horse-shoe flanked on the left with pliers and on the right a hammer. This appeared to be the general pattern of plates for farriers, although variations have been seen from contemporary paintings. The edging of the plate and the horse-shoe pliers and ornaments are in white metal.

Uniform

Farriers wore single-breasted blue coats with white tape button holes in threes on both sides. The skirt and cuffs were buff material, which was seen when the coat was worn turned back. The coat had red collar patches with a button and tape on both sides. The sides, cuffs and back of the coat were decorated in white tape 'V' with a button in the centre of each. A white stock was worn, and the coat buttoned at the neck and fell away. A buff waistcoat was worn, bound and looped with white tape. Buff breeches were worn, buttoned to above the knee with white knee protectors. Black boots with reinforced tops cut at the back were worn with steel spurs. A brown leather apron was worn and, as in the illustration, was rolled up across the front. Buff gauntlets were worn.

Accoutrements

A white buff belt was worn over the left shoulder with a brown leather pouch on the right hip. A large, rolled valise at the front on the saddle contained all the necessary tools, spare horse-shoes, nails, pliers and so on. The axe was carried. The housings were buff and decorated on the hindquarter with the letters XI D surrounded by foliage. The cape was worn rolled at the rear.

Weapon

Axe. Farriers have carried the axe from the earliest days of cavalry. The purpose of this weapon was the execution by a 'coup de grace' of any horse that was so maimed in battle as to be of no further practical use to the regiment. This was achieved by the provision of a sharp, broad-bladed weapon with a short shaft and heavy head.

7. 15th Light Dragoons. Trooper, 1759

Head Dress

The helmet worn by the 15th Light Dragoons is now known as the Emsdorf helmet. It was a skull jockey cap with comb and turned-up peak. The skull was black, japanned copper with a white metal foliage on each side. The comb was fluted white metal with a medusa head at the front. The peak was in black, japanned steel turned up and edged in white metal beading. The comb had a red horse plume falling down on the right-hand side. The turban worn by the 15th was scarlet cloth tied in a bow at the back and hanging down, ending in silver tassels. The turban was bound with white metal chain. The design on the front peak was a large Garter belt with the motto *Honi soit qui mal y pense* surmounted by a crown. Inside the Garter was a lion. On each side were trophies of the regimental Guidon and Bourbon flags. The shell at the base bore the words *Merebimur*, and below the flags on each side the words 'At Emsdorf'.

Uniform

The regiment was raised in 1759 as Elliot's Light Dragoons. The facing colours at this time were green and did not change to blue until 1766 for their gallantry in the Seven Years War. The coat itself was of red cloth, lined in white. On the collar there were 2 strands of white worsted lace with buttons. Down the front of the coat were 5 rows, each of 2 strands of lace, each strip of lace ending in a silver button. The lace was mounted on blue lapels terminating at waist level. The epaulettes were of green cloth edged with white and fringed on the end. On the forearm of the coat, stretching from just below the elbow to the edge of the green cuff, were 2 pairs of white worsted lace 'V's with a button in the centre of each. The same pattern appeared on the coat tails on each side, and above the rear vent. The coat was worn unbuttoned over a white waistcoat with two pockets. A black stock was worn. The breeches were white, buttoning at the knee, and black leather boots rose above the knee in the front and dipped at the back with steel spurs.

Accoutrements

The crossbelts, 2 in number, were of white, buff leather, one passing over the left shoulder with carbine swivel and black pouch, and the other over the right shoulder terminating at the left in a sword frog.

Light Dragoon troopers also carried a billhook, which, although designed for gathering fodder, was undoubtedly also used as a weapon.

Weapons

Weapons of the Light Dragoons at this period were a sword, a pair of pistols and a carbine.

Sword. The sword had a plain brass knucklebow and leather-bound grip, and the blade was approximately 37 in. long. The 15th Light Dragoons carried a straight sword, but other regiments had either curved or straight swords, depending on regimental regulations. The sword was carried in a leather scabbard with top and bottom mounts, and was normally suspended from a shoulder-belt which went over the right shoulder.

Carbine. The carbine was a flintlock weapon with a barrel 36 in. long and having an overall length of 4 ft 3 in. A bayonet was also carried, having a blade of some 12 in. The carbine was fitted with a bar and sliding ring attached to a swivel, which could move up and down the shoulder-belt, carried over the left shoulder. When

not on the shoulder-belt, the carbine was carried in a bucket fastened to the rear of the saddle.

Pistol. The pistol carried was of 24 bore with a barrel 10 in. long, the grip and fore end being of one piece of walnut, and the butt cap being of brass with long ears running up the sides of the grip. The ramrod pipe was also of brass, and the weapon was fitted with a flint pistol lock. The pistols were carried in a pair of holsters fitted over the pommel of the saddle.

8. 2nd Dragoon Guards. Trooper, 1760

Head Dress

The head dress worn at this period was similar throughout the Dragoon and Dragoon Guard regiments of the army. It was a black felt hat with a wide brim, looped up on all 3 sides, forming the well-known three-cornered hat or tricorne. In the case of the 2nd Dragoon Guards, the brim was bound all round with yellow braid. The officers' hats were trimmed with gold braid. On the left side was a black silk bow or rosette with a regimental-pattern button in the centre.

Uniform

The uniform shown in the illustration was that worn during the campaign against the French. The regiment was ordered abroad in the early spring of 1760 and had its first skirmish with the enemy on 10 July, at Corbach.

The tunic was a long red coat, extending below the knee and worn with the front skirts turned back to reveal the lining, which was of the buff facing material. There was no collar, and the tunic was worn open with the lapels buttoned back, exposing a white waistcoat and a white stock. The buttons were grouped in threes on the front of the tunic with yellow worsted lace buttonholes. Large cuffs of buff colour with buttons and taping completed the tunic. Buff shoulder straps were worn, and a yellow cord aiguillette on the right shoulder. Buff breeches were worn, with white stockings and heavy, black dragoon boots.

Accoutrements

A large white, buff crossbelt was worn over the left shoulder with a buff leather pouch containing carbine ammunition and certain items of necessity. The shabraque was rounded at the back end and was buff in colour. A broad yellow stripe of about 4 in. was placed around the edge with a 2-in. centre stripe of scarlet. Holster covers of buff material with the same edging as the shabraque were worn around the brown, leather pistol holsters. The embroidered crest on shabraque tail and pistol holsters was the crown above a circular Garter with motto *Honi soit qui mal y pense* in yellow on a blue background, and on the centre was the Royal cipher G.R. on a scarlet background. A leather carbine butt bucket was worn on the right fore of the saddle. Horses had their tails docked.

Weapons

Sword. In the middle of the eighteenth century Heavy Cavalry carried a basket-hilted back sword with a long, straight blade, terminating in a spear point, the hilt being very much akin to the Venetian schiavona and the Scottish basket-hilt. Depending upon the regiment, these were in either steel or brass, and although giving full protection to the hand, tended to cramp and restrict the exercises that could be performed with the sword.

Scabbards were mostly of leather, with a metal top-mount and chape, the top-mount bearing a stud so that the sword could be carried slung from the shoulder in a baldrick.

There were many variations of hilt piercing, depending upon the regiment and the particular whim of the commanding officer.

Pistol. In addition to the sword noted above, troopers carried the land service pistol. This was a weapon with a 12-in. barrel of 17 or carbine bore, the bulbous butt having a long-eared brass cap, brass trigger guard and ramrod pipe; the furniture being of walnut. The lock was the standard flint carbine lock, the entire weapon being some 18–20 in. in length.

9. 16th Light Dragoons. Trooper, 1776

Head Dress

The helmet worn by the 16th Light Dragoons from 1759 until 1780 had a triangular plate on the front in black japanned steel, on which appeared an oval with crown above.

The oval contained the Garter motto *Honi soit qui mal y pense* in a large letter C, being the cipher of Queen Charlotte. Encircling the lower edges of the oval was a laurel-leaf pattern and scroll on both sides of the crown, bearing the inscription 'The Queens'. The plate was fixed on to a leather skull which had a black turban encircling the bottom of the helmet, then tied at the rear in a bow. The helmet was topped by a red horsehair plume from a crest with white-metal fittings. On the front of the comb was a medusa head. Down each side of the helmet were white-metal reinforcements to give added protection to the head from sword cuts.

Uniform

The scarlet coat was worn with black facings until 1766, but after that, for their conduct in America, the regiment wore Royal blue facings to their coats. On the collar there were 2 strands of white lace with a silver button of regimental pattern. The taping on the lapels and buttons on the taped buttonholes, were arranged in pairs in 5 groups. The shoulder cords were white lace with white fringes. Above the blue cuffs, which had a 'V' going downwards in the front, were 4 rows of white lace, also in a 'V' shape, with silver buttons on each. These 'V's were grouped in pairs. The coat was worn unfastened over a white waistcoat with two pockets at the waist. A black stock was worn. The back of the tunic had a centre vent which was turned back and buttoned down to reveal the white lining. There were 4 rows of white lace in 'V's with a button in the centre going down each turnback. At the top of the centre vent were 2 pairs of lace on each side, the top two having silver buttons. The blue collar widened and fell at the back of the neck in a 'V' shape. The trousers were of white material and the boots of black leather, rising above the knee in the front, but having a drop of 5 in. at the back to enable the wearer to bend the knee. Steel stirrups and spurs were worn.

Accoutrements

The crossbelts were of white buff leather, one passing over the left shoulder with carbine swivel and black ammunition pouch, and the other over the right shoulder, terminating at the hip in a sword frog.

Weapons

The weapons of the Light Dragoons at this period were a sword, a pair of pistols and a carbine.

Sword. The sword had a plain brass knucklebow and leather-bound grip, and the blade was approximately 37 in. long. The 16th Light Dragoons carried a straight sword, but other regiments had either curved or straight swords, depending on regimental regulations. The sword was carried in a leather scabbard with top and bottom mounts and was normally suspended from a shoulder-belt which went over the right shoulder but, in some Light Dragoons, the sword was carried slung from a waist-belt.

Carbine. The carbine was a flintlock

weapon with a barrel 36 in. long and having an overall length of 4 ft 3 in. A bayonet was also carried, having a blade length of some 12 in. The carbine was fitted with a bar and sliding ring attached to a swivel, which could move up and down the shoulder-belt, carried over the left shoulder. When not on the shoulder-belt, the carbine was carried in a bucket fastened to the rear of the saddle.

Pistol. The pistol carried was of 24 bore with a barrel 10 in. long, the grip and fore end being of one piece of walnut, and the butt cap being of brass with long ears running up the sides of the grip. The ramrod pipe was also of brass, and the weapon was fitted with a flint pistol lock. The pistols were carried in a pair of holsters fitted over the pommel of the saddle.

10. 17th Light Dragoons. Trooper, 1790

Head Dress

The helmet worn was common to all Dragoons and known as the tarleton. It was low at the back of the head and was basically a leather skull with large black leather metal-bound peak. The turban, which was bound with silver chain, was white and a 14-in. high red-and-white feather plume was fitted into the socket behind the turban on the left side. The turban tied in a bow or knot at the rear under the bearskin crest which surmounted the helmet. On each side of the skull was a metal strip to give added protection to the

wearer against sabre cuts. On the right-hand side of the helmet was placed the regimental badge, and across the front, above the peak, a band of metal bearing the title of the regiment, 17th Light Dragoons. No chin scales were worn, but black tapes were fitted to be tied either round the chin as shown or round the back of the neck to keep the helmet firmly on the head.

Uniform

A blue jacket with white collar and cuffs was worn. The jacket was frogged down the front with white worsted cord, according to the pattern laid down for each regiment. The cuffs were edged and trimmed with white cord as well. The jacket was cut to just below the waist and ornamented round the bottom and up the back seams. A crimson sash was worn around the waist. The breeches were of white leather or kerseymere and fastened below the knee; black knee-length boots and steel spurs completed the outfit.

Accoutrements

A white buff leather crossbelt and black pouch were worn over the left shoulder and around the waist a black leather waist-belt with 3 sabre-tache slings and 2 sword slings. The sabretache was of black leather with a pocket behind, and in silver bore the badge of crossbones, surmounting a skull, beneath which was a scroll of the regimental motto 'Or Glory'. The shabraque was a plain blue court pattern pointed at the hindquarters with a tassel at the end.

The pistol holsters were worn at the front, covered with black lambswool.

Weapons

Sword. The sword carried was the light dragoon sabre pattern of 1788. This had a steel stirrup hilt with languets on both sides above and below the crossguard. The grip was of wood lapped with string and then covered in thin leather. The slightly curved blade was fullered along the back edge and terminated in a hatchet point. It was carried in a heavy steel scabbard with two rings for sling suspension.

Pistol. Troopers also carried a flint-lock dragoon pistol which was first introduced in 'Regulations for Clothing & Appointments, etc.' for 1756. This was described as 'a pistol of 10 in. the barrel and of carbine bore'. It had a steel barrel, walnut wood furniture, brass trigger guard and ramrod pipe. The butt was protected with a heavy brass cap.

11. Royal Horse Artillery. Officer, 1793

Head Dress

A light dragoon tarleton was the helmet ordered for the 2 troops of Royal Horse Artillery A and B on their introduction into the British Army in 1793. The helmet was crowned with a bearskin crest and had a crimson turban tied round the helmet and tied in a bow at the rear. A white plume was worn on the left side (although some contemporary prints show no plume worn). General Mercer recollects that the first pattern turban may have been of leopard skin, but notes that, in 1797, he recollects officers with crimson turbans. The helmet was straight at the back. The peak was hard, black leather edged in gilt brass trim and, above, a band bearing the words 'Royal Horse Artillery'. There were no chinstraps or chin scales on this pattern helmet. On the right of the helmet was a gilt brass badge consisting of a circle surmounted by a crown. The circle was edged with a Garter with the words 'Royal Regt. of Artillery' and in the centre a Royal cipher of GR. The helmet had two brass strips on each side, as was the pattern with all light dragoon helmets towards the end of the nineteenth century, and thus afforded protection against sabre cuts.

Uniform

A blue, light dragoon, pattern coatee was worn with red collar, cuffs and turnbacks. The coatee fastened at the neck and sloped away, revealing a white waistcoat. The lapels and cuffs had gilt buttons of special pattern of a norman shield with 3 cannon balls in line above 3 cannon placed vertically facing left in a shield, as shown in the illustration. The coatee had thin 'Y'-shaped epaulettes sewn on backing of regimental face colour. The waistcoat of white kerseymere was fastened with gilt regimental-pattern buttons. A crimson waist sash was torn tied and knotted with hanging tassels on the left-hand side. The breeches were white kerseymere or doeskin and black, light dragoon pattern boots raised above and cut low behind the knee so the wearer was able to bend the knee.

Accoutrements

A white buff crossbelt was worn over the right shoulder with 2 sword slings, 1 long and 1 short. It was joined on the chest with an oval, gilt belt plate bearing the arms of the ordnance, 3 cannon balls and 3 cannon and the words 'Royal Artillery'. The shabraque was plain blue with a line of gold russia braid running round the edge about 2 in. in. The holster of brown leather, containing a pair of pistols, was covered in lambskin.

Weapon

Sword. General Mercer, in his *Military Reminiscences*, says, 'In the Horse Artillery, besides a large regulation sabre, we had a small undress one, usually so crooked as to be useless for anything but a reap hook.' The regulation sabre for Horse Artillery at that time was the light cavalry weapon with a stirrup hilt in steel, a wooden grip covered in leather with a steel backpiece with 2 ears which protruded around the grip. The blade was curved, $32\frac{1}{2}$ in. from shoulder to point around the curve, and terminated in a hatchet point. The sword was carried in a heavy steel scabbard with 2 loose rings for sling suspension. Most officers' blades were decorated by being blued for half their length and engraved with the Royal cipher, the Royal coat-of-arms and other decoration, the engraving being filled with mercurial gold.

12. 16th Light Dragoons. Officer, 1793

Head Dress

The helmet, or tarleton as it was known, was worn by all Light Dragoon regiments at this period. It was a leather skull with a black, hard-japanned leather peak. The helmet was surmounted by a fur, bearskin crest. The turban, contained by silver chains, was black silk, tied at the rear in an ornamental bow under the rear of the bearskin crest. The peak was edged in metal with a titled band above the peak over the front of the skull. Two metal bands were fixed, one each side, to give added protection to the wearer from sabre cuts. The band across the front gave the title '16th Light Dragoons'. On the left side was a plume in cut feathers of white over red, affixed in a socket beneath the turban. On the right side was worn a regimental-pattern badge surmounted by a crown. The helmet had no chin scales at this period, but was fitted with black leather tapes which tied beneath the queue at the rear.

Uniform

A blue jacket, to below the waist in blue cloth, was worn with red collar, cuffs and turnbacks. The front of the coat was frogged with silver lace with 3 rows of buttons, and the undercoat of blue was also fully frogged. The collar and cuffs were edged and ornamented in silver lace, and the turnbacks were also edged in silver. The epaulettes were of blue, edged in silver, with silver-edged red lining. A black stock was worn and a white ruffle. Pelisses were worn about 1780–81, and they were fur lined. It is interesting to note that officers of the 16th were permitted to have upper jackets (top coats) lined in leopard skin, but in 1786 this permission was rescinded. The underjacket was, in fact, the waistcoat of the uniform, but with sleeves, and from 'Rules & Regulations for the Sword Exercise of the Cavalry, 1796', it appears to have been used as an undress jacket for drill purposes. The back of the coat was embroidered with silver lace ornaments both sides of the vent. The underjacket was clearly shown in 'Rules & Regulations for the Sword Exercise of the Cavalry, 1796', with a trefoil of lace ending in smaller trefoils both sides. The front of the underjacket was fully frogged and squared off at the bottom and top like a plastron. The breeches were of white kerseymere buttoning below the knees. The boots were of black leather with reinforced tops, and steel spurs were worn.

Accoutrements

A white buff crossbelt over the right shoulder with 2 slings, 1 on the left hip and 1 at the middle of the back, was worn, and the sword suspended from there attached the weapon to the wearer. The belt was attached to the chest by a rectangular plate of regimental design. The holsters and saddle had a black lambskin cover and the cloak, rolled on the back of the saddle and lined in red, was rolled with the red outermost.

Weapon

Sword. Pursuant to the order of 1788, officers of Light Dragoons carried the same sword as their troopers. This sword, which is shown in detail in 'Rules & Regulations for Sword Exercises of the Cavalry, 1796', had a curved blade with a ramrod back (i.e. of circular section), and the hilt was steel stirrup with languets on both sides protruding both up the blade and grip. The grip was of wood, to which was moulded a covering of leather which, when put on wet, dried in the exact shape of the wooden former. The backpiece was of steel. It was carried in a heavy steel scabbard with two rings for sling suspension.

13. 10th Light Dragoons. Trooper, 1794

Head Dress

The helmet worn at this period was the standard light dragoon pattern known as a tarleton. It was low at the back of the head and had a turban of yellow silk, being the facing colour, and was surmounted by a bearskin crest. The peak of the helmet was in hard, black leather bound round the edge with a gilt brass edging. The turban was bound with silver chain. The helmet had, on both sides, a gilt brass metal strip to give added protection against sabre cuts. A gilt band across the front of the leather skull gave the name of the regiment, 'Prince of Wales or 10th Light Dragoons'. A yellow plume was worn in a socket beneath the turban, on the left side. On the right side a large silver Prince of Wales feather badge was worn. The helmet had no chin scales, although black tapes were fitted to tie beneath the queue at the rear.

Note: A painting of this regiment at Windsor Castle shows a leopard-skin turban for 1795–96.

Uniform

A blue shell jacket with yellow collar, cuffs and turnbacks was worn. The illustration shows a trooper wearing over this jacket the regulation cloak, which was blue-grey in colour and had a short cape attached at the collar which was yellow. The jacket was blue and frogged on the front in white worsted lace according to regimental pattern. The coat was worn with the top few buttons fastened and sloping away to reveal its blue undercoat. The shoulder straps on the jacket were yellow, edged in white with blue rings edged in white. The back of the underjacket, which was cut to below the waist and not as a shell jacket, was ornamented with white worsted cord. The jacket had the yellow turnbacks edged in white lace with white loops in pairs on the back, both sides, and an inverted 'V' at the top of the vent. The breeches were white leather or kerseymere and fastened below the knee. Black knee boots, with extra protection at the top but cut away

at the back, were worn with steel spurs.

Accoutrements

Two white, buff crossbelts were worn. A black leather ammunition pouch, on which was fitted a carbine swivel, was attached to the one over the left shoulder. The crossbelt over the right shoulder ended in a sword and bayonet frog on the left hip. The housings were yellow, edged in white and yellow and bearing the crest of the Prince of Wales on a red background within the Garter at the hindquarter and the holster covers.

Weapons

Sword. The 1788 pattern light dragoon sabre was carried. This had a stirrup hilt in steel with thin languets both above and below the crossguard. It had a flat-topped pommel and plain backpiece, and the grip was of wood knurled with string and then covered with leather. The blade was slightly curved, fullered at the back edge and terminated in a hatchet point. It was carried in a scabbard of steel with rings for sling suspension.
Carbine. A 'specification of arms' issued by Ordnance in April 1794 listed the light dragoons carbine as a weapon with a barrel of 28 in. This was a flintlock carbine of musket bore with woodwork in walnut and with brass butt plate, trigger guard and ramrod pipes. A considerable number of these were made by Henry Nock, who held the contract for at least 500.
Pistol. The light dragoon pistol, introduced in 1759, had a 9-in.

barrel, flintlock action and was stocked up in walnut. The butt cap, trigger guard and ramrod pipes were in brass.

14. Shropshire Provisional Cavalry. Trooper, 1794

Head Dress

This was a leather tarleton light dragoon pattern helmet with a bearskin crest. It was low at the back of the head, and the turban was in black silk bound with silver chain. Two silver ribs were fitted to both sides of the helmet, from the fur crest to the turban. These were added as extra protection against sabre cuts. The peak was edged by a silver band, and the front of the helmet had a band naming the troop of Provisional Cavalry. The plume, 14 in. in length, was worn on the left side from a socket under the black silk turban. A black tape was fixed to each side, tying behind the queue, and this kept the helmet in place on the head. It is interesting to note that a letter, signed by the Duke of Portland on 26 November 1796, and written to the Lord Lieutenant of Shropshire gives the recommended uniform and the 'leather cap and feather' were priced at 2s. 6d.

Uniform

The jacket, recommended by the Duke of Portland and subsequently adopted, was a green, hip-length tunic edged in white with scarlet collar, cuffs and lining. The front of the tunic was turned back when mounted, revealing the scarlet lining piped in white. Ten rows of white, worsted lace bars with knots at the ends and silver ball buttons decorated the front. The collar was tall and open at the front to show a white stock. Collar and cuffs were edged with white. The back of the jacket was laced and pleated from the waist. White twisted cord epaulettes were worn, and the price was given as 19s. The breeches were green with a dark welt, priced at 10s. and the black leather boots with turned tops cost 18s.

Accoutrements

The sword baldrick or crossbelt was in white, buff leather with a pair of slings suspended from the left side on the hip, for the sword. The belt was joined on the chest with an oval, silver belt plate with the regimental device engraved upon it. A rolled cape was carried behind the saddle, and the horse's tail was cut short. A black lambskin was worn across the horse in front of the saddle, over the pistol holsters.

Weapon

Sword. The pattern of sword carried by the Provisional Cavalry was the 1788 pattern light dragoon sword. This had a plain knucklebow in steel, and the grip was of ribbed leather with an all-steel backpiece.

The guard had narrow languets extended above and below the crosspiece, preventing an opponent's sword blade from cutting the hand if it should slide down the blade that far. The blade was slightly curved, terminating in a hatchet point, and it was carried in a steel scabbard with rings at the mouthpiece and approximately 8 in. down the scabbard.

The majority of these swords were manufactured by Thomas Gill of Birmingham, J. J. Runkel of Solingen and Woolley of Birmingham.

15. 4th Dragoons. Officer, 1807

Head Dress

The head dress worn by the officer in the illustration was the full-dress cocked hat of black beaver or felt. A black silk rosette was fitted on the left side with a loop of silver lace and a regimental-pattern button. Each corner of the hat was decorated with silk, oak leaf pattern, black bands. Gold and crimson hat pulls were fitted at each end. A white over red feather plume was fitted behind the black silk rosette.

Uniform

The coat was single-breasted with 8 flat bars of silver regimental-pattern lace, grouped in pairs. The turnbacks were blue, as were the collar and cuffs. The blue was lighter than Royal blue. The tails were fastened by a button. Two loops of silver lace were on each end of the collar, which opened at the front to reveal the stock. The cuffs for Dragoons were square and edged in lace. The epaulettes, when worn, were of linked chain, but the illustrations show silver-cord shoulder straps. The breeches were of white kerseymere or doeskin, and black boots with steel spurs completed the dress. White gauntlets were worn.

Accoutrements

A silver lace crossbelt was worn with buckle slide and tip, the lace having two blue silk trains at each end. An embroidered pouch was fitted to the crossbelt at the centre of the back. The waist-belt was of white buff with gilt plate with GR surmounted by a crown and scrolls and motto beneath in silver. Two sword slings and 3 sabretache slings were fitted on the left side. The housing was red edged with regimental-pattern lace and with the regimental-pattern device on each hindquarter, and crown and device on the holster.

Weapon

Sword. Pursuant to an Order of 1788, officers carried the sword as ordered for private men. This was the pattern of 1796, and consisted of a straight-bladed sabre of some $1\frac{1}{2}$ in. wide and 35 in. long, terminating in a hatchet point. The guard was a disc of sheet steel metal pierced with circular holes about its periphery. The knuckle-bow was a continuation of the guard. The grip was a wooden former covered in leather, and the backpiece in plain sheet steel had 2 ears which enveloped the centre of the grip. The scabbard, of steel, was heavy and strong and was equipped for sling suspension.

16. 7th Hussars. Officer, 1807

Head Dress

The full-dress helmet worn by the 7th Hussars and illustrated in our picture was a tall tapering shako with no peak. The cap had the upper portion covered in light blue cloth, and the lower part was of black. A silver, lace edged 'streamer', ending in a gold bullion flounder and tassel, hung from the right side as shown. Corded gold lines were fixed to the cap on the right side. The badge, worn on the black part at the front, was of gold or crimson lace in a cockade. A white over red, cut feather plume was worn at the top front of the shako. The shako was called a mirleton or flügelmutze. The cap was most decorative and was worn also in plain black leather with a turned-up peak at the front in service dress, and was called a 'watering' cap.

Uniform

The Hussars, who had been converted from Light Dragoons, still retained their white facing collars with the new hussar jacket. The jacket was of dark blue cloth, fully frogged on the front. The uniform, which was the light dragoon uniform, was authorised in 1785 and was the same in 1807 with a few minor exceptions. The jacket was a short waist-length sheer jacket with an open high collar to reveal the black stock and white ruffle (if worn). The jacket was single-breasted with 3 rows of buttons. The middle row had ball buttons and the 2 outer rows half-ball buttons. The centre row of buttons, of silver and of regimental pattern, numbered 16 and the 2 outer rows numbered 29. The cuffs and collar were decorated in twists and scrolls and knots of silver russia braid. The back was ornamented down the seams and round the bottom of the jacket with russia braid. Chain epaulettes were worn in certain orders of dress. The breeches were of white buckskin or kerseymere and were worn with silver-trimmed hessian boots. A dolman or pelisse was worn in blue cloth with the same pattern of silver frogging but edged round the cuff, collar and lower edge with light brown fur (the other ranks having white). A crimson and gold barrel sash was worn around the waist, tying at the back, from which cords and acorns attached at the front.

Accoutrements

A gold lace crossbelt with silver buckle slide and tip. The gold lace sword belt had 2 wide slings for the sword and 3 narrower slings for the sabretache. The sabretache was of white facing colour in leather. The whole was edged in wide gold lace and in the centre had a crown and Royal cipher below. The pouch was a leather box with the flap of same design as the sabretache in the embroidered devices. The shabraque was in white facing colour edged all round in wide gold lace and with bullion tassels at the points of the hindquarters' tails. The crown with cipher below appeared on both tails and front holster covers. The seat cloth was of white lambskin.

Weapon

Sword. Officers of Dragoon, Lancer and Hussar regiments, when in full dress or levee dress, carried a levee sword. This was a mameluke-hilted scimitar with a hilt in ivory and a gilt crossguard. It had a curved blade and was normally carried in a leather scabbard with gilt mounts. However, each regiment had its own regimental pattern, which affected the style of crossguard and scabbard mounts, some of these being extremely intricate, others being very plain, and it would take a whole book to describe each and every one of these.

17. 6th Dragoon Guards. Officer, 1808

Head Dress

The head dress shown in the illustration was the full-dress cocked hat. The cocked hat was in black felt. A black silk lace rosette was fitted to the left of the hat with a loop of silver lace and a small regimental-pattern button. The corners of the hat were decorated with bands of black silk lace of oak-leaf pattern. The hat was bound with black silk lace round the top. There were gold and crimson hat pulls at each end of the hat to which strings were attached which, when pulled or slackened, tightened or loosened the headband. A white over red feather plume was fixed behind the black silk rosette.

Uniform

The coat was single-breasted and almost identical in style to that of the Dragoons, with 10 loops of regimental silver lace grouped in pairs. The lace was 6 in. wide at the top and 4 in. wide at the bottom. The turn-backs were lined in white kerseymere and edged in silver lace; tails were fastened by buttons; collars and cuffs were of white cloth with two loops of silver lace at either end and edged in thin silver lace. The cuffs had 2 pairs of silver 'V' loops on the sleeve with a button in the centre of each. The epaulettes were of linked chain and marked on 'Y' shape of material of regimental face colour. This was padded beneath to give added protection against sabre cuts. A black silk stock was worn. The breeches were of white doeskin or kerseymere and black boots with reinforced tops were worn with steel spurs. White gloves or gauntlets were worn, depending on the order of dress. In service dress the overalls were of blue material with stripe down the outside seam, and they fastened with buttons.

Accoutrements

A white buff waist-belt with two sword slings, one long and one short, was worn, fastened at the front with a regimental or universal pattern buckle of brass plate, with crown and GR with motto below and with palm leaves on either side. A white buff crossbelt was worn with gilt, brass buckle slide and tip and with a black leather pouch.

Weapon

Sword. Heavy Cavalry officers at this period should have been carrying the same sword as their troopers. The Heavy Cavalry trooper's sword at this period was the pattern of 1796, having a flat guard in the form of a disc pierced with round holes. The knucklebow was the continuation of the disc in sheet steel; the backpiece, in steel, had two ears overlapping the grip, which was of wood bound with lines of thin cord and then covered with moulded leather to form a non-slip panel. The blade was straight, 35 in. long, terminating in a hatchet point, and it was carried in an exceptionally heavy scabbard with two loose rings for sling suspension.

18. 6th Dragoons. Officer, 1810

Head Dress

The shako shown in the illustration was generally known as a 'watering' cap. It was made of black leather and measured about 10 in. high. In the front was a detachable square peak also of leather. The chin scales were of brass, laid one on top of the other to give a scaled effect and were attached to the cap by a large brass roundel. The caplines were of gold cord. On the front of the cap there was an 8-pointed star in silver with the castle of Inniskilling raised in the centre and below, completely separate from the star, a large 6 D in silver. The plume on the top front of the shako was of white over red cut feathers.

Uniform

The uniform was single-breasted in scarlet cloth with 10 loops of regimental-pattern lace down the front grouped in pairs. They measured 6 in. wide at the top and 4 in. wide at the waist. The turnbacks were lined in yellow kerseymere and were edged in lace according to regimental custom, the tails being ornamented with the regimental button. The collar and cuffs were of yellow cloth, the collar having 2 rows of loops on each side and the cuffs had 2 pairs of 'V'-shaped loops in pairs with a button in the centre of each 'V'. The epaulettes were of linked chains and were padded to protect the wearer against blows aimed at the shoulder. Black silk stock was worn at the neck. The breeches were of white buckskin, but on active service these were discarded and grey overalls were worn. The boots were of black leather and were cut low at the back of the knee.

Accoutrements

The waist-belt was of white, buff leather with a rectangular brass plate of regimental pattern. On the left side there were 2 brass rings to which 2 sword slings were attached, also in buff leather. The crossbelt was of white, buff leather with a black leather pouch attached, which was worn at the back so it hung down to the waist.

Weapon

Sword. Officers carried the same sword as their troopers, in pursuance of an order of 1788. This was the famous disc hilt which had a thin sheet knuckle bow and a large circular disc pierced around the perimeter. The grip was of wood, bound with string and then covered with thin leather, and the plain backpiece had 2 ears which protruded around the grip and were riveted to it. The guard also had 2 strong languets protruding for about $1\frac{1}{2}$ in. down the blade, which was 35 in. from shoulder to point, $1\frac{1}{2}$ in. wide at the shoulder and almost parallel to within 4 in. of its hatchet point; it was carried in a very robust steel scabbard with 2 rings for sling suspension.

19. 6th Dragoons. Officer, 1811

Head Dress

The illustration shows an officer in service dress, or campaign dress, uniform. Again, another variation of head dress of the Dragoons and Dragoon Guards was worn. It was a plain black 'watering' cap or flügelmutze. A false front peak was worn turned up. The cap was shaped at the bottom to fit the head. Silver caplines encircled the cap, hanging down on the right side, ending in flounders. A white metal star badge was worn on the front. A round white metal rosette was fitted to the top centre of the cap, behind which was a plume holder. The plume was a tuft of feathers of white over red.

Uniform

The uniform at this period was the usual single-breasted scarlet coatee.

The collar was high and of yellow with 2 broad bands of silver lace at each end. The front was decorated in 10-in.-wide bands of silver lace, replacing in 1811 the previous narrow bands. Also, the skirts were made shorter. The turnbacks were lined in yellow, as the face colour. The cuffs were in yellow with two 'V's of regimental-pattern lace with a button in the centre. One 'V' was in the yellow face colour and one was above it. The epaulettes were of linked chain and were padded to give extra protection from sword cuts. They were backed on the regimental face colour of yellow. A scarlet waist sash was worn. Buff overalls were worn with a silver stripe with a blue train in the centre down both outer seams. The bottoms were protected with buff leather. White gauntlets were worn.

Accoutrements

A white buff waist-belt was worn with silver snake fastening and with two slings.

Weapon

Sword. Officers carried the sword that was later carried by Heavy Cavalry officers in 1822. This had a straight blade some 32 in. long and terminating in a double spear point. The hilt was in gilt brass and consisted of a knucklebow and a pair of boat-shaped shells. The grip was invariably bound in silver wire, and the pommel was spherical. The scabbard, in steel, had a strong steel shoe and was equipped with two rings for suspension from slings.

20. 10th Hussars. Trooper, 1812

Head Dress

The head dress shown in the illustration is a busby adopted by regiments that were converted to Hussars from Light Dragoons at the turn of the nineteenth century. The busby was of light brown fur with a white over red osprey feather and with a red bag or fly, as it was termed, on the right side. This fly was without yellow bullion. The caplines were of yellow cord, with flounders and tassels hanging down on the left side. The lines came from the left side under the fly, fastened around the neck and hooked on the uniform. The chin scales, when worn, were of gilt chain, but heavily ornamented, backed with velvet of the face colour. It is interesting to note that shakos were introduced for some Hussar regiments in 1812, but busbies continued to be worn at Waterloo because of the delay in supplies arriving from Britain.

Uniform

The 10th had been converted into Hussars from Light Dragoons in 1806 owing to the particular interest His Royal Highness, the Prince of Wales, took in the appearance and condition of the regiment. Richard Cannon goes on to add that the Prince of Wales procured His Majesty's consent for its being clothed and equipped as Hussars. The 10th changed their facing colour from yellow to red in 1794, when the new blue light dragoon uniforms were introduced. The jacket was of blue and fully frogged on the front. The jacket was short to just below the waist, with a red collar and cuffs, the collar being open at the front, revealing a black stock. The jacket was single-breasted with 5 rows of buttons, the centre being ball buttons and the outer row being half-ball buttons. The cuffs had an edge of white, worsted and decorated above, with white worsted lace. The collar was edged in white lace and ornamented. The pelisse was of similar design to the jacket, but edged all round the collar and cuffs in white worsted, and around the bottom and the base of the side seams in the same material. The breeches were white leather buttoned below the knee with black hessian pattern boots dipped at the front.

Accoutrements

A white buff crossbelt and black leather pouch was worn with carbine swivel for attaching to the gun, the belt having a brass buckle slide and tip. A barrel sash of crimson and yellow cord was worn, fastening at the back, and with the crimson cord and yellow acorns hanging from the front right. A white buff waist-belt and slings for sword and black plain leather sabretache attached to the left hip was on the left side. The saddle cloth was red edged in white pattern with the Royal cipher on hind and forequarters. The seat cloth was white lambskin, and the roll behind the saddle bore the letters X above LD on each end.

Weapon

Sword. Light Cavalry troopers of 1812 carried the sword pattern of

1796. This was a stirrup hilted sword with languets on the crossguard, a heavy steel backpiece with ears overlapping the grip, which was of wood covered in leather. The blade was curved and terminated in a hatchet point and measured round the curve $32\frac{1}{2}$ in. from shoulder to point, its width being $1\frac{5}{8}$ in. at the shoulder. It was carried in a heavy steel scabbard with 2 loose rings.

21. Royal Horse Guards.
Officer, 1814

Head Dress

The helmet was of black japanned or lacquered metal. The front plate was gilt brass with a crown and GR reversed cipher with decorated edge. The plate had a straight top which rose to just below the gilt brass crest, on to which was affixed a red and dark blue-black worsted comb. The peak of the helmet was either all gilt brass or sometimes covered in black leather with a gilt brass edge. On the left side of the helmet a white over red feather plume was worn in a square gilt brass plume holder. The highly ornamented chin scales were gilt and attached to the helmet by ornamental bosses on each side and tied under the chin. This pattern of helmet was replaced with the Roman style in about 1817.

Uniform

A blue short jacket with scarlet collar, cuffs and turnbacks. The high collar was open at the neck, revealing the black stock. The collar was edged all round in regimental-pattern lace of gold with a scarlet silk train. A gold gorget tab was worn on each end. Both sides of the front of the single-breasted jacket were lined with a broad band of regimental pattern, the jacket fastened by being hooked up. A waist girdle of gold and scarlet was worn with tassels on the right front. The turnbacks on the short-tailed jacket were red, edged in gold lace and sewn back without button or ornament. The cuffs were gauntlet pattern of scarlet, again edged in gold regimental-pattern lace. The shoulder was fitted with twisted gold cords. The overalls were sky blue with a double gold lace stripe with a sky blue light between. The boots were black with gilt spurs.

Accoutrements

A gold lace crossbelt with gilt buckle slide backed with scarlet leather was worn over the left shoulder and a red leather box pouch with scarlet flap, edged in gold lace and with a crown above a Garter star superimposed on a trophy of arms and flags. The sword belt was gold lace with gilt regimental-pattern buckle. Two sword slings and 3 sabretache slings were fitted to the belt. The sabretache was gold lace edged and the same design as the pouch and was embroidered in the centre. The shabraque was red edged in gold lace and fringed with the same design as the sabretache on each hindquarter with the letters RHG below. The holster covers were also of red, edged in gold lace and fringe, with the crown, Garter star and trophy of arms. The flaps were red with gold lace and fringed edge and a crown and GR embroidered in the centre.

Weapon

Sword. Officers of Life Guards and Royal Horse Guards were equipped with an elaborate sword that had no previous history in the British Army. The pommel was ball shaped in gilt brass, and the grip was spirally shaped in wood covered in leather and bound with 3 gilt wires. The guard was cast in scroll and bore on the outside a cartouche which consisted of a crown surmounted by a lion 'passant gardant'. The blade was straight, 35 in. long and had a double fuller for its entire length. It was equipped with a brass reinforced leather scabbard with provision for sling suspension.

22. Royal Horse Artillery. Officer, 1815

Head Dress

The head dress was the light dragoon pattern of leather with gilt-rimmed peak and blue-black velvet turban bound with gilt chain. The peak was rimmed with gilt and had a band on the front with the words 'Royal Horse Artillery'. A 14-in. white plume was worn on the left side and on the right were battle honours on two scrolls. These were personal honours awarded to the man and not the regiment. The comb which surmounted the helmet was covered in black bearskin. The sides of the helmet were reinforced with gilt ribs to ward off sabre cuts. Gilt chin scales were worn attached to the helmet by large gilt rosettes. These were tied beneath the chin. The turban was tied at the rear under the bearskin comb in a large bow.

Uniform

A blue, short shell jacket was worn with red collar and cuffs with 24 bars of gold cord and 72 gilt buttons, although a certain latitude seems to have been allowed on the number of bars of gold worn on the breast of the tunic. The collar was worn open, revealing the stock and edged in gold cord. The cuffs were edged with gold lace in a pointed pattern. The tunic had 3 rows of buttons, 1 down the centre and the other 2 rows at the extremities of the bars of cord. A crimson waist sash was worn around the waist, knotted with hanging tassels at the right front. White doeskin breeches were worn with buttons at the knees and gold-trimmed levee boots with gold tassels. The back of the jacket was ornamented with gold cord.

Accoutrements

A sword belt was worn under the sash. Two sword slings, one long and one short, in white buff, suspended the sword on the right side. The saddle cloth was blue with gold tassels at the hindquarter at the end of the pointed tail. These tails were weighted. A rolled valise was worn behind the saddle.

Weapon

Sword. The pattern of sword carried by officers was to be the same as used by their private soldiers, i.e. a stirrup-hilted sabre, but it was notable that commanding officers insisted on a slightly more elaborate version. The hilt was slightly lighter than the regulation, and the curved blade was decorated for at least half its length by being blued and having gold-filled engraving which normally incorporated the Royal coat-of-arms, the Royal cipher, a trophy of cavalry arms and a foliate pattern. A large number of these swords were made by J. J. Runkel of Solingen, in Germany, but English makers included Woolley & Deakin and Thomas Gill.

In addition, officers of the Royal Horse Artillery carried a dress sword with a very curved blade and a mameluke-styled ivory hilt. This was, of course, useless as a fighting weapon and was purely decorative.

23. Royal Horse Artillery (Rocket Troop). Gunner, 1815

Head Dress

The head dress was still the light dragoon pattern helmet, adopted on the forming of the Royal Horse Artillery in 1793, but with modifications. Basically, it was a leather helmet with peak and a bearskin comb. The helmet had a black silk turban bound with brass chain, and it had the back shaped to the head. A 14-in. plume was worn in a socket under the turban on the left side and a brass badge on the right. The comb on the helmet was

slightly enlarged, as a contemporary account states that the regimental collar maker improved the comb by using the combs of the old-pattern helmet. Brass chin scales held by gilt rosettes on both sides were worn. These chin scales, when not worn under the chin, were worn tied up at the back under the bearskin comb. The black turban tied in a bow under the comb at the rear.

Uniform

A blue, short shell jacket was worn with 24 bars of yellow worsted cord with 72 buttons. The collar and cuffs were red, lined with yellow cord, with a pattern on the collar and small knot on the cuffs. Yellow worsted shoulder cords, being twisted, were worn. The jacket dipped slightly at the back, but not long enough to be tails. The edge of the skirt was edged in yellow cord. The collar was open at the front, revealing the black stock. Blue-grey overalls were worn with a broad scarlet stripe and brass buttons in the centre of the stripe. The overalls were booted or lined with brown leather on the inside of the leg and around the bottom. The back of the jacket was piped in yellow worsted cord, as the Royal Horse Artillery.

Accoutrements

A white buff crossbelt and black leather ammunition pouch was worn with brass buckle slide and tip on the belt. A waist-belt of white buff was worn, on which was suspended a brown leather pistol holster on the left hip. The saddle cloth was blue edged in yellow lace with the crown and Royal cipher on the hind-quarter ending in a point with a tassel. The holsters at the front had the crown and Royal cipher. Under the holster were carried the Congreve rockets, either 2 $\frac{1}{2}$-lb rockets or 1 1-lb rocket. The poles for the rocket were carried in the holster on the right side and had a pennon, as the illustration shows. Rolled blankets and valise were worn behind the saddle.

Weapons

Sword. The weapon carried was the 1796 pattern for Light Cavalry troopers. This was a stirrup-hilted sword with ears on the backpiece overlapping the grip, which was covered with leather over a ribbed wooden former. A buff sword knot was tied to the pommel end of the knucklebow. The blade was curved and terminated in a hatchet point, the total length of the sword being 37$\frac{1}{2}$ in. It was carried in a heavy steel scabbard with 2 loose rings, the total weight being approximately 5 lb. These weapons were mainly made by Gill of Birmingham and Woolley & Deakin, although some may be seen bearing the name Dawes.

Pistol. The pistol carried by this regiment was a double-barrelled side-by-side weapon with 1 barrel rifled and the other true cylinder bore. The length of the barrels was 18 in., and their calibre was 13 balls to the pound. The barrels were browned, and the stock, which was of walnut, had steel furniture and steel rammer.

On top of the barrels was fitted a folding elevating sight. The weapon was supplied with a detachable butt which could be fitted so that it could be used in the manner of a carbine. The sole maker of these weapons was Henry Nock, and they are extremely rare collectors' items.

Rocket. Each man carried on his saddle 2 Congreve rocket heads, and the sticks for these were carried on the right side of the saddle and were invariably decorated with a blue and-white pennon.

24. 2nd Dragoons Officer, 1815.

Head Dress

A black, bearskin cap, peculiar to this regiment in the Dragoon and Dragoon Guards, was authorised for the regiment to wear on 19 December 1768 by Royal Warrant. The first pattern introduced was similar to the cap worn by Grenadiers. The cap had a large gilt plate bearing the Royal coat-of-arms. This plate was virtually covered by the fur hanging down in the front. At the rear of the cap was a red material patch, round in shape with the white running horse of Hanover. The caplines were of gold twisted cords and tassels which encircled the cap and ended in the cords and tassels hanging on the right side. A white plume in cut feathers came from a plume socket on the left side of the cap. Brass chin scales were attached to the cap on both sides. A black leather peak was attached to the front.

Uniform

A scarlet coatee, with high Prussian collar and open at the front to reveal the stock, was worn. The coatee had dark blue collar, cuffs and turnbacks. On each side of the collar and, continuous down the front of the coatee, were 2 broad bands of gold lace with a dark blue line through the centre of each. This pattern of lace came round the collar and edged the turnbacks. The turnbacks were fastened by a regimental-pattern button which was surrounded by a gold-embroidered rosette on a circle of cloth of the regimental face colour. The shoulder straps were scarlet cloth edged with yellow lace and held with a gilt brass regimental-pattern button. The coatee was hooked up down the front. The overalls were of blue-grey material at the bottom with brown leather and with a blue stripe piped in dark blue-black down each edge of both legs' outside seam. The illustration shows the undress overalls of blue-grey with yellow stripe and not the service-dress overalls as described. A cummerbund waist girdle was worn buckled on the inside and fixed on the outside with gold loops and olivets.

Accoutrements

A white, buff leather crossbelt with gilt buckle slide and tip was worn with a black leather pouch; also a white, buff waist-belt with two sword slings and three sabretache slings. The buckle was gilt brass with a white metal crown, GR and laurels and a scroll with motto. The sabretache was plain, black patent leather with 3 brass rings. The shabraque was blue, edged in gold lace with blue train with a crown and GR reversed, with the letters R.N.B.D. denoting Royal North British Dragoons. The roll on the rear of the saddle was scarlet with the same initials in gold embroidery. White buckskin gauntlets were worn. A scarlet blanket roll was worn over the front of the saddle. In service dress the haversack of white linen and the round wooden water-bottle was worn.

Weapon

Sword. Heavy Cavalry officers at this period should have been carrying the same sword as their troopers. The Heavy Cavalry trooper's sword at this period was the pattern of 1796, having a flat guard in the form of a disc pierced with round holes. The knucklebow was the continuation of the disc in sheet steel; the backpiece in steel had 2 ears overlapping the grip, which was of wood bound with lines of thin cord and then covered with moulded leather to form a non-slip panel. The blade was straight, 35 in. long, terminating in a hatchet point, and it was carried in an exceptionally heavy scabbard with two loose rings for sling suspension.

25. 1st Life Guards. Officer, 1817

Head Dress

The helmet introduced for the Life Guards, both 1st and 2nd, in 1817 was of the Roman style, as shown in Dighton's drawings. The skull, peak, front and back, and comb were of white metal. The skull was ornamented on both sides with sprays of laurel leaves starting at the back band and flowing out towards the front. The peaks were bound with gilt brass trim. The chin scales were extremely ornately decorated and were attached to the helmet at each side with large gilt lionheads. The chin scales tapered slightly to a fixing under the chin. The front plate was of sunray pattern and gilt, with a large coat-of-arms on the plate with the Prince of Wales' feathers behind. The comb was edged in a scalloped gilt brass trim, and to this was attached a large bearskin comb.

Uniform

The coatee was of scarlet cloth with blue collar, cuffs and turnbacks. Turnbacks were blue and fastened with a gilt button and embroidered ornament. The collar was decorated with two bands of regimental-pattern lace with extra embroidery at the ends on both fronts of the collar. The cuffs were square and decorated with lines of embroidery terminating in a button. The cuirass worn was of polished steel and edged in gilt brass with studs all round the edge. It was lined with velvet, which showed at the arm holes, neck and waist, and was blue. The cuirass was edged at the front, which dipped low with gilt brass scalloped pattern trim. On the front of the cuirass was a large, gilt, sunburst star which was worn until about 1825. The shoulder scales were scales terminating on the chest in embroidered ends. Epaulettes in gold bullion were worn, although those

illustrated, together with the aiguillettes were not the usual forms worn. The overalls were of claret mixture colour with double gold stripe down the outer seam of each leg. The order for the introduction of the claret mixture overalls came from the Prince Regent in February 1817, when it was also ordered that the double-breasted coatee previously worn was to be replaced by a single-breasted one.

Accoutrements

A gold lace crossbelt was worn over the left shoulder, backed on red morocco leather with gilt buckle slide and tip. The pouch was a box pouch with blue velvet flap edged in gold lace and decorated with the crown above the Garter star superimposed on a trophy of arms and flags. The waist-belt worn, under the cuirass but on the coatee, was gold lace with gilt buckle and with 2 sword slings and 3 sabretache slings. The sabretache was blue leather covered in blue velvet and edged in gold lace. In the centre was the Garter star on the trophy of arms and flags, above which was a crown surmounting a ribbon scroll with the battle honour. Below the star and trophies were two crossed sprays of laurels, and under these another ribbon scroll with battle honours. The honours were PENINSULA and WATERLOO. The shabraque was blue with crown above GR surrounded on top by a scroll on both hindquarters and the holster covers. A lambskin seat cover was worn. The shabraque was edged with gold lace with a light between.

Weapon

Sword. Officers of Life Guards and Royal Horse Guards were equipped with an elaborate sword that had no previous history in the British Army. The pommel was ball shaped in gilt brass, and the grip was spirally shaped in wood covered in leather and bound with 3 gilt wires. The guard was cast in scroll and bore on the outside a cartouche which consisted of a crown surmounted by a lion 'passant gardant'. The blade was straight, 35 in. long and had a double fuller for its entire length. It was equipped with a brass-reinforced leather scabbard with provision for sling suspension.

26. Light Horse Volunteers. Trooper, 1817

Head Dress

The helmet was a leather tarleton light dragoon pattern, crowned with a bearskin crest. It was low at the back, and the turban which, until 1803, had been of scarlet silk, was now black moleskin fur, with bands of silver chain. A badge, as shown in the illustration, was worn under the fur crest on the right side of the helmet, above the turban. On the left side of the helmet a white on red, cut feather plume 14 in. long was worn, the plume coming from under the turban from a hidden socket. Silver rosettes and chin scales were worn. The peak of the helmet was edged with a silver band, and on the front was a ribbon with the words 'Light Horse Volunteers'. The turban was tied in a bow at the back under the fur crest. This

helmet was discontinued in 1820 in favour of the newly introduced cavalry shako.

Uniform

The jacket worn at this period was of scarlet cloth, with black velvet collar and cuffs. The cuffs were ornamented with silver cord Austrian knots, and the collar was edged with silver lace and small loops of silver and russia braid. The front was richly embroidered with 18 rows of silver lace in the hussar fashion, with 3 rows of silver ball buttons. The back was embroidered, with lace up the seams edged in silver russia braid and terminating in crow's-foot pattern below the level of the arm. The jacket was of the shell-jacket pattern, pointed at the back. Twisted silver cord epaulettes were worn on the shoulders. Overalls were in light grey mixture with a broad silver lace stripe.

Accoutrements

A silver lace crossbelt with silver buckle, slide and tip, and black patent-leather pouch was worn. The badge worn on the pouch was as shown in the illustration. The waistbelt had a silver snake fastening. Belt, sword slings and sabretache slings were of silver lace. The sabretache was in black patent leather with the badge in silver, as shown in the illustration. Dress Regulations of 1804, when the patent leather sabretache was adopted, states, 'A black patent leather sabretache was adopted instead of that of bearskin, which was found to suffer from the ravages of moth.' A black cloth shabraque was worn, edged in scarlet, and with a 2-in.-wide silver lace stripe all round.

Weapons

Sword. The Light Horse Volunteers were equipped with a light cavalry sword, pattern of 1796. This had a heavy stirrup hilt with wide languets, a ribbed, leather-covered grip and the steel backpiece had 2 ears which protruded around the back of the grip and were riveted to it. The blade was slightly curved and terminated in a single spear point, and the sword was carried in a heavy steel scabbard with rings at the mouthpiece and some 9 in. down the scabbard.

This was the weapon which the English Light Cavalry used to such good effect at Waterloo, and in its basic form it remained in service with the Light Cavalry until 1829.

Pistol. This regiment was armed with the 1796 pattern light dragoon pistol. It was a flintlock weapon with a short rounded butt and plain walnut furniture, and carried a smaller version of the standard musket lock. It had an all-metal ramrod and was of musket bore.

27. 2nd Life Guards. Officer, 1820

Head Dress

The bearskin was of brown fur 20 in. high with a large gilt plate sunrayed at the base on the front with the Royal arms and regimental badge raised upon it. Below the plate there was a black leather laquered peak.

At the top of the cap was a gold bullion tassel from which a gold plaited cord came, passing over the left side of the cap and fastened on the right side with a gold flounder and bullion tassel. The chin scales were of gilt brass ornamented to regimental pattern. At the bottom left of the bearskin there was a large, gold embroidered grenade. Hidden behind this was the gilt socket in which a white leather plume 2 ft long was fitted, running up the side and over the top of the cap.

Uniform

The coatee was of red cloth with blue velvet collar, cuffs, skirts and turnbacks. All these except the turnbacks were heavily embroidered with oak-leaf pattern in gold wire. The epaulettes were of gold bullion, on which was embroidered the regimental device. Aiguillettes led from the right epaulette which hooked up at the neck from a catch on the top of the cuirass. The cuirass of back and front plate was steel lined with red leather and edged with gilt brass trim and brass domed studs. A blue velvet crimped edge showed all round. A blue belt with 3 lines of gold held the cuirass at the waist. The overalls were crimson with a broad gold lace stripe of regimental pattern. Gauntlet gloves were worn in review order. The shoulder scales of the cuirass were of gilt brass on leather and fastened on to a stud on the front. The ends were gold embroidery on dark blue velvet. The cuirass was waisted and pointed at the front, dipping low.

Accoutrements

A gold lace crossbelt of regimental pattern was worn with a gilt buckle slide and tip. The pouch was embroidered in review order. The crossbelt showed an edge of dark blue velvet. The sword belt worn under the cuirass showed only the slings in gold on dark blue velvet. The shabraque was blue, edged in wide gold lace edged with a red border on the inside. On the hindquarters was a large gold embroidered grenade. Over this was worn a dark sheepskin saddle cover edged with a red vandyked border.

Weapon

Sword. The sword carried by officers at this period was possibly the most elaborate that they were to carry in their entire history. The gilt brass openwork guard was richly decorated with a foliate pattern, and on the outside it bore a cartouche, surmounted by the crown and containing in a wreath a similar crown, surmounted by a lion 'passant guardant'. The grip was of leather, bound with 1 strand of gilt wire, and the hilt was surmounted by a flattened, spherical pommel. The blade, which was single-edged, long and straight, had 2 fullers separated by a rib which continued for the full length of the blade from hilt to point. It was carried in a black leather scabbard, ornamented with a brass openwork sheath which covered it from mouthpiece to chape and was equipped with 2 rings 8 in. apart for suspension.

28. 4th Light Dragoons. Officer, 1820

Head Dress

A black beaver bell-top shaped shako was worn, 8 in. deep with a sunken black leather top 11 in. in diameter. A band of 2-in. leaf-pattern silver lace was fixed around the top of the shako, and black silk ½-in. binding around the bottom. The badge was embroidered, with GR reversed in the centre surrounded by the Garter and decorated with rose, thistles and shamrocks. The whole badge was on a black velvet ground. Engraved silver-plated scales were worn tied together in front above the leather peak of the shako. The scales were held to the sides of the shako by lionheads. The scales were also worn above the plume holder and were connected with lionpaws. Rich and dead gold cord caplines encircled the cap at the top and bottom, tied in a double knot on the right side and passed through a ring; from there, they went around the body and hooked up, ending in gold acorns. A black leather chinstrap was fitted. The plume was white and red falling feathers, held in a gilt socket on the front of the shako.

Uniform

A blue cloth coatee was worn with a plain 3-in. Prussian collar of regimental face colour and a 4-in. deep pointed cuff. Turnbacks and linings were also of facing colour, in this case yellow. Light dragoon skirts were 7 in. in length and 6 in. at the bottom, and were decorated with slashed pleats and 3 buttons. The back seam and welts of the jacket were in the facing colour. A plastron on the front with 9 buttons was worn, and the jacket fastened by hooking up down the centre. A silver, lace-fringed backpiece was worn on the back of the tunic at the top of the skirt. A gold-and-crimson waist girdle was worn fastening underneath with a strap and buckle and decoratively fastened on the outside by gold loops and olivets. Silver lace strap and bullion epaulettes were worn, the bullion being $2\frac{1}{2}$ in. in length and with bullion crescents. Ranking was worn on the epaulettes. The overalls were sky blue with a wide stripe of silver lace up each outward seam.

Accoutrements

A silver lace pouch belt with scarlet train in the centre was worn. The pouch was black leather with a large silver flap with crown and GR reversed fixed in the centre. The waist-belt was silver lace on morocco leather with scarlet train fastening in front with snake ornament. Two side slings for the sword and 3 narrower slings for the sabretache completed the belt. The sabretache was faced with blue cloth. It was 14 in. deep, 12 in. wide at the bottom and $8\frac{1}{2}$ in. at the top. It was edged with 2-in. silver lace all round, leaving a welt of blue. The centre was a GR reversed cipher with crown and scroll above and scrolls and laurels either side and below, with the regimental battle honours. The shabraque was blue, edged with silver lace, with scarlet train and with crown and GR reversed at the front, and a crown GR reversed and battle

honours on the tail. The seat cloth was white.

Weapon

Sword. Pursuant to an order of 1788, cavalry officers should have been armed with the same sword as their troopers, and in the main this was so, although officers' swords tended to be more ornate. The weapon had a stirrup hilt in steel, with steel back-piece, and the grip was covered in leather. The wide blade was $37\frac{1}{2}$ in. long and had a distinctive curve. The majority of these blades were heavily blued and gilt, with a pattern which included a trophy of cavalry arms, the Royal coat-of-arms within the Garter and the Royal cipher. It was carried in a heavy steel scabbard with two loose rings for sling suspension.

29. 9th Lancers. Officer, 1820

Head Dress

The lance cap worn at this period was much taller and heavier than that of the late nineteenth century. The top was made of cane, covered in crimson cloth, and was crossed with gold cord. The sides were of crimson cloth to the slight waist in the cap above the body. A boss on the left side at the top was in gold looped wire over a wooden former with crimson velvet centre embroidered with G.R. cipher. At the waist, between the cloth and the patent-leather body, there was a zigzag pattern gold lace band with a crimson centre line. The patent-leather body had a false peak at the back, edged in gold lace, 1 thick and 1 thin row, and the peak at the front had the same 2 lines of lace. The cap plate was a large gilt sunray plate with the Royal arms in the centre. The chin scales were worn across the sunray plate, hooked up on to a lion-head boss on the right-hand side of the top of the cap. It is interesting to note that the undress lance cap also had a crimson top, but the whole cap was smaller and plainer. There was no lace on the peak and no sunray plate or chin scales. Both caps carried white over red cock's feather plume, worn behind the boss in a gilt holder.

Uniform

The short-tailed coatee was of blue cloth with crimson stand collar embroidered with gold lace; it had crimson lapels buttoned back, and the jacket was fastened with hooks and eyes. The skirt was short, being 5 in. long with crimson turnback and buttons. Gold bullion fringe hung at the back waist. The girdle was gold and red. A gold lace sword sling and sabretache belt with snake fastening were worn. The overalls for full dress were crimson with a broad gold lace stripe. The tunic cuffs were crimson, pointed and edged with gold lace. Gold cord caplines were of lancer pattern. Epaulettes were gold.

Accoutrements

The crossbelt was gold lace with crimson train. Buckle slide and tip were of silver, and the silver pouch had gilt ornamentation; chains and pickers were worn on the belt. The sabretache was of purple leather with

blue cloth edged in lace with embroidery of crown and reversed **GR** cipher.

Weapon

Sword. The pattern of sword carried by officers was to be the same as for their private soldiers, i.e. a stirrup-hilted sabre, but it was notable that commanding officers insisted on a slightly more elaborate version. The hilt was slightly lighter than the regulation, and the curved blade was decorated for at least half its length by being blued and having gold-filled engraving, which normally incorporated the Royal coat-of-arms, the Royal cipher, a trophy of cavalry arms and a foliate pattern. A large number of these swords were made by J. J. Runkel of Solingen in Germany, but English makers included Woolley & Deakin and Thomas Gill.

30. 6th Bengal Light Cavalry. Officer, 1825

Head Dress

The undress head dress was a cap in dark blue cloth with a very broad top, which had a button in the centre. The peak was of black leather edged in silver lace. The chinstraps were of plated scales and were worn tied up above the peak. They fitted to the cap by means of lionhead bosses.

Uniform

A short stable jacket of French grey cloth, fastening down the front by means of hooks and eyes. Two stripes of silver lace about $1\frac{1}{2}$ in. in width down the front both sides of the fastenings. The collar was red, edged all round with silver lace. The cuffs were pointed and also of red cloth and measured about 4 in. from the point to the edge of the cuff. They were edged in silver lace. The bottom of the jacket was edged in 1 in. silver lace. The welts and back seams were piped in red cloth. The trousers were of dark blue cloth, the inside leg reinforced with leather. A thick stripe of silver lace ran down the side seams of the trousers with a thin stripe of red each side.

Accoutrements

The sabretache was faced with dark blue cloth backed in dark blue leather and with the usual pocket at the back. The front was edged with a $2\frac{1}{2}$-in. band of silver lace, according to regimental custom. In the centre was the number VI over the letters BLC. Under these initials were 3 scrolls bearing the battle honours LASWAREE, SITABULDEE and BHURTPORE. All these devices were embroidered in silver lace. The sword belt, slings and sabretache sling were of silver lace, the waist-belt having a snake fastening.

Weapon

Sword. Officers carried the sword pattern 1822 with a 3-bar steel hilt, including a chequered top piece which continued into the backpiece, and this was again chequered for some 2 in. above the guard. The grip was of fish skin bound with 3 silver wires.

The blade was slightly curved, and was $32\frac{1}{2}$ in. from shoulder to point and $\frac{7}{8}$ in. wide at the shoulder. It was carried in a steel scabbard with top and middle rings, and the overall length of the sword was approximately 38 in.

31. Royal Horse Artillery. Officer, 1828

Head Dress

The shako worn by officers of the Royal Horse Artillery dated from the abolition of the light dragoon or tarleton pattern helmet on 22 December 1827. The shako was bell-shaped and $6\frac{1}{2}$ in. deep, with a black, glazed leather top slightly sunken, $11\frac{1}{2}$ in. in diameter. There was a band of glazed leather around the top and bottom of the shako. The one at the bottom had a small buckle at the back. Leather 'V's from the top to bottom band were sewn on the shako on both sides. Gilt scales were worn tied up over the plume holder in the top centre of the shako, and a patent-leather strap was worn under the chin. The caplines were plaited gold cord. They were attached from a ring on the left side of the top and laid down over the peak end up the other side to a loop; from there two cords came down and attached to the right upper chest of shell jacket, ending in flounders and tassels. The plume was white falling pattern 10 in. high and held in a large gilt holder. The plate was a gilt star and in the centre surmounted by a crown and star circled with laurels, 3 cannon horizontally.

146

Uniform

A dark blue shell jacket with red collar and cuffs was worn. The collar was edged in gold lace and cord. The cuffs were ornamented with cord and gold russia braiding. There were 20 rows of ball buttons down the front of the shell jacket with an equal number of gold cord bars looped at the ends and joined. The back of the shell jacket was embroidered and ornamented, as the lancer pattern, down the back seams. The overalls were light blue of the cossack pattern and as worn by Light Dragoons, and edged down the outside seam with a broad, gold lace stripe. A gold and crimson barrel sash was worn around the waist, with the crimson cord and acorns looping up to the right front.

Accoutrements

A gold lace sword belt was worn with regimental-pattern buckle with two wide sword slings to support the sword and three small slings to suspend the sabretache. The sabretache was of blue facing and edged in a wide band of gold lace and with the crown and Royal cipher in gold on it. The shabraque was blue with large gold lace edging piped on the outer seams in red and with tassels on either end of the pointed hindquarters. The seat cloth was black lambskin with a red edge vandyked.

Weapon

Sword. Officers carried the sword pattern 1822 with a 3-bar steel hilt, including a chequered top piece which continued into the backpiece; this was again chequered, for some 2 in. above the guard. The grip was of fish skin bound with three silver wires. The blade was slightly curved, and was $32\frac{1}{2}$ in. from shoulder to point and $\frac{7}{8}$ in. wide at the shoulder. It was carried in a steel scabbard with top and middle rings, and the overall length of the sword was approximately 38 in.

32. 8th Hussars. Officer, 1828

Head Dress

The head dress worn by Hussars and Light Dragoons at this period was a bell-shaped black beaver shako. The hussar pattern was $8\frac{1}{2}$ in. deep and with a $10\frac{1}{2}$-in. diameter black, sunken glazed top. Around the top of the shako was a line of narrow looping of gold russia braid, and in the centre was a wheel of gold embroidery, communicating by a chain loop with a regimental button to a large royal cord rosette at the top. The shako had a black, patent-leather peak in front and a turned-up one at the back, both edged with french braid. The chin scales were attached to each side of the shako by rosettes and fastened beneath the chin. The plume was a black, drooping cock's feather from a gilt socket at the top of the shako. The caplines encircled the body of the cap twice. They were suspended on either side by a lionhead ring, tied to the right side and hung with gold acorns and loop which fastened two buttons on the jacket.

Uniform

The shell jacket was of blue cloth with a 3-in.-deep Prussian collar, laced round and ornamented with russia braid. The jacket was single-breasted with 5 rows of buttons, the centre row being ball buttons and the other 4 rows half-ball buttons. The jacket was richly embroidered across the chest with chain loops of dead gold gimp and the effect relieved by a looping of light russia braid. The cuffs were pointed about 3 in. deep and laced round with regimental-pattern lace with extra russia braid ornamentation. The edges of the jacket were richly interlaced with russia braid around the regimental lace, which passed over knots at the back. The welts and side seams were also ornamented with russia braid. The jacket had a white silk lining. The pelisse was of the same pattern as the jacket, except that it had a 4-in.-deep collar, covered in grey astrakhan, and also grey astrakhan around the cuffs and around the bottom of the pelisse, with inlets to the seam and welts. The pelisse had a crimson silk lining. Gold-plated necklines with acorns and slides were worn with the pelisse. The overalls were blue with a broad gold stripe of regimental pattern.

Accoutrements

The pouch belt had 1½-in. white gold lace with scarlet cloth edging and morocco lining with a gilt buckle slide and tip attaching to a scarlet cloth pouch edged with gold embroidery and with a double GR in the centre surmounted by a crown. The sabre-tache was scarlet morocco 15 in. deep, 9 in. wide at the top and 13 in. at the bottom with a 2-in. gold lace around the outside edge and embroidered on the scarlet cloth in the centre was a GR reversed surmounted by a crown. The waist-belt, which was also of gold lace backed on scarlet morocco, had three narrow sabretache slings ½ in. wide and two sword slings ¾ in. wide.

Note: The pouch illustrated in the picture is of the 8th Royal Irish Hussars, but came in at a later date than the uniform depicted. It has been shown here to illustrate the deviations in the design of pouches from that laid down in Dress Regulations. These designs crept in even more later in the century, and in later Dress Regulations they are referred to as 'to be of regimental pattern'.

Weapon

Sword. Officers carried the sword pattern 1822 with a 3-bar steel hilt with a chequered top piece which continued into the backpiece. This was also chequered, for some 2 in. above the guard. The grip was of fish skin bound with three silver wires. The blade was slightly curved and was 32½ in. from shoulder to point and ⅞ in. wide at the shoulder. It was carried in a steel scabbard with top and middle rings, and the overall length of the sword was approximately 38 in.

33. 5th Dragoon Guards.
Officer, 1831

Head Dress

The large roman-style head dress shown in the illustration was worn by all Dragoon and Dragoon Guard regiments from 1822, when it was introduced, up until 1831, when it was replaced by a similar helmet, but all in gilded brass. The skull, peak and comb, were of black glazed leather (although examples have been found in metal, but Dress Regulations of 1822 only state black glazed). The skull was ornamented on both sides with gilt laurel sprays. The peaks were bound with gilt brass trim. The chin scales were ornately stamped and tapered to the fixing point under the chin. They were attached to the helmet with large gilt lionheads. The plate on the front was of sunray pattern and gilt bearing the Royal coat-of-arms, beneath which was a scroll with the regimental number and name, '5th or Princess Charlotte of Wales Dragoon Guards'. A large black bearskin crest was worn.

Uniform

The coatee was scarlet with collar cuffs and turnbacks of regimental face colour, in this case blue. The coatee was single-breasted with 8 buttons. The Prussian collar was 3½ in. deep, laced with lace loop and small button at both ends. The skirts of the Dragoons were rounded with 4 laced loops and buttons, 2 buttons at the middle of the back, at the waist. The skirts were decorated with embroidered ornaments according to regimental pattern. The cuffs had laced loops and buttons. White gauntlet gloves were worn, as in the illustration. The overalls were of blue-grey with a 1¾-in. lace stripe up each outside seam, of regimental pattern. The epaulettes were of gold bullion.

Accoutrements

The crossbelt was 2¼-in. gold lace lined with morocco leather with edging of blue-velvet. The gold lace was of regimental pattern. A gilt buckle slide and tip completed the belt. It was attached to the pouch box, which was blue leather with a velvet-covered flap edged with lace and a blue-velvet edge. A gold embroidered G.R. surmounted by a crown and relieved by silver encircled with oak leaves was worn on the flap. The sword belt consisted of gold lace with blue-velvet edge, with regulation gilt plate, burnished silver GR and crown encircled with oak leaves. The sword slings and three sabretache slings were attached on the left side. The sabretache was of blue morocco leather edged in lace and covered in blue-velvet with gold embroidered GR and crown relieved in silver and encircled with leaf. The foul-weather cover of morocco was lined in green baize. The shabraque was blue edged in gold with embroidered cipher and regimental number on hindquarter.

Weapon

Sword. Officers carried the sword pattern of 1822, which had a brass knucklebow and boat shells. The hilt

149

was in fire gilt brass and the grip completely covered in twisted silver wire. The narrow straight blade, 1⅛ in. wide at the shoulder, was 33 in. from shoulder to point and had a flat back and 1 fuller along the back edge from shoulder to point and another wide centre fuller which ran to within 6 in. of the point. It was carried in a black leather scabbard with 3 gilt mounts, the top and middle mounts having rings for sling suspension.

34. Worcestershire Yeomanry. Officer, 1832

Head Dress

A black beaver bell-top shako of the same dimensions as the regular cavalry was worn with black patent-leather top and black patent peak. The shako had a band of black lace around the upper edge and a black leather band around the base. A white, falling horsehair plume (surgeons and farriers having a black plume) in a gilt socket was worn. A gilt crown and star plate badge was affixed to the front of the shako. Gold cord caplines encircled the bell-top shako twice (although a variety of methods of wearing these is noted from Richard Dighton's drawings). All show them hooked up on the side from an ornamented fitting. The chin scales were gilt, attached from gilt rosettes and worn hooked up over the plume socket. A black, patent-leather chinstrap was worn. (The shako for other ranks cost just over 11s. 5d.)

Uniform

A scarlet coatee was worn by the Worcestershire Yeomanry, who were raised in April 1831. Various troops of cavalry had existed, but were lapsed by 1828. A scarlet coatee was adopted because of William IV's insistence on scarlet. The coatee had a Prussian collar and cuffs of buff facing material with no lace edging. The coatee was double-breasted with gilt buttons of regimental pattern. Silver lace, bullion-boxed epaulettes were worn, that is to say with the bullion tassels fixed to a former card, not loose. A gold-and-scarlet waist girdle was worn. Caplines were worn on the body with gold flounders. Dark blue-grey overalls with a broad red stripe were worn.

Accoutrements

A white, japanned leather crossbelt with black patent pouch was worn, the pouch belt having gilt buckle slide tip and chains and pickers. A black leather waist-belt and sword slings with gilt fittings were worn.

The shabraque was dark blue, square end to the front, and with pointed ends at the rear edged in silver lace. The saddle cover was in white lambswool edged in scarlet cloth.

Weapon

Sword. Officers carried the 1822 pattern light cavalry sword with a 3-bar hilt in steel, which was decorated to improve the grip. The sword was 38 in. overall, the blade being 32½ in. from shoulder to point and 1 in. wide at the shoulder. It was carried in a steel scabbard with 2 rings 8 in. apart for suspension from sword slings.

35. Aide-de-Camp to the King, 1834

Head Dress

The following head dress was worn by the aide-de-camp to King William IV. It consisted of a cocked hat, 12 in. high, and worn 'fore and aft'. One side (the left, as worn) was slightly higher than the right. The hat was made of black beaver, bound with black oak-leaf pattern lace at each corner on the right side The right side was decorated, also, in the centre, with gold bullion embroidery and netting. At each end of the hat, in the turn-ups, were crimson and gold bullion hat pulls which, in former days, were tied to the laces in the brow band and, when pulled, tightened it. The plume was of white cock's feathers and was worn in a socket on the right of the hat, but down over, to envelop the top of the hat, and it hung down each side.

Uniform

The scarlet coatee had blue face cloth collar and cuffs. White turnbacks joined at the base with gold-embroidered oak leaves and button. The collar was deep, being 4 in., and embroidered all around with gold oak-leaf wire. The coatee was single-breasted and decorated with 7 rows of gold, oak-leaf embroidery. The tails had 3 buttons on each side with gold oak-leaf embroidery button-holes. Cuffs were slashed and had 3 buttons on heavy, gold oak-leaf-pattern embroidery. Gold bullion epaulettes were worn, with deep coiled fringe. Aiguillettes in plaited gold cord were worn from the left shoulder. The overalls were of blue with 2-in., oak-leaf-pattern, gold lace stripe. Brass box spurs were worn.

Accoutrements

A gold, oak-leaf-pattern waist-belt and sword slings were worn. The clasp was a gilt plate with the Royal cipher and crown in silver. The shabraque was of blue cloth, square at the front and slightly pointed at the rear. The shabraque was edged with a blue welt and 2-in. gold lace stripe, with red train. The crest embroidered on the tails and wallets was the crown over Garter with the Royal cipher in the centre on scarlet cloth. A palm-leaf spray decorated either side. The horse tackle was black leather with brass fittings and martingales.

Weapon

Sword. In 1834 a special sword was ordered for all staff officers. This was derived from the 1822 pattern general officers' sword and had a gilt brass Gothic hilt with a cartouche bearing the rank badge of a major-general, i.e. crossed swords and baton within a wreath. It had a slightly curved blade and was carried in a brass scabbard.

Dress Regulations ordered that it be carried by all staff officers, aides-de-camp and inspectors of militia, and it remained in service for these officers until approximately 1900.

36. Royal Horse Guards.
Officer, 1834

Head Dress

The bearskin was of black fur 14 in. deep in the front with 5½-in. gold bullion tassels hanging from the centre of the right side. A gilt grenade was worn in the front partially hidden by the fur, with the Royal arms raised in the centre. Gilt chin scales were worn attached to the bearskin cap by lion-head rosettes. These were clasped according to regulation by a small rose of the same pattern, under the chin. A red feather 24 in. in length, made of swan feather, was fixed in the left side and curved upwards over the cap, as in the illustration.

Uniform

The coatee was of blue cloth with red collar, cuffs, skirts and turnbacks. All these except the turnbacks were heavily embroidered. The collar was a Prussian collar, 3½ in. deep, with the embroidered loop and button at each end. The skirts were of dragoon pattern with buttons with embroidered loops and buttons. The turnbacks had a white lining, with embroidered ornaments on the tails. Gold aiguillettes with 2 sets of chain loops came from the right epaulette, and ran across the breast and suspended from a hook at the neck of the cuirass. The cuirass itself was polished steel edged in brass with domed studs all around. The cuirass dipped at the waist and was held by a belt of white buff leather. The shoulder straps were gilt brass scales with cut steel facets and terminated in silver lionheads at each end on the front of the breast. The overalls were blue with broad stripe of regimental-pattern lace. Gold epaulettes were worn on both shoulders, with bullion fringes and richly embroidered straps showing a scarlet cloth edge.

Accoutrements

A white, leather sword belt with sword and sabretache slings in white buff. The crossbelt was white buff with buckle slide and tip in gilt brass. The crossbelt had a flask cord in scarlet passing through loops in the centre of the belt. The pouch was black patent leather, ornamented on the flap, with a gilt oval plate bearing the King's arms. The belt was fastened to the cartouche box by small straps and buckles. The sabretache was of blue leather and was faced with blue and edged in wide gold lace. On the centre was a Garter star surrounded by gold embroidered trophies and regimental badge. The whole was surmounted by a crown. This was suspended by two slings of white buff. The shabraque was scarlet with an edging of rows of gold lace bearing a blue light between. The covers were embroidered with a crown and Garter star with scrolls with the words PENINSULA and WATERLOO.

Weapon

Sword. The sword ordered for the officer of the Royal Horse Guards in Dress Regulations of 1834 was similar to that authorised for the 1st and 2nd Life Guards in the same year. It had a heavily chased pommel ornamented on the back with a Tudor rose, and the guard, which was of 3 chased and scrolled bars, had a wide turndown at the back ornamented on both sides with a crown. The blade was straight, some 32 in. long with a single edge, and was 1⅛ in. wide at the shoulder and tapered to a hatchet point. It was carried in a steel scabbard with 3 ornate gilt mounts, the chape being very heavy and the middle and top mounts being fitted with suspension rings.

37. 15th Hussars. Officer, 1834

Head Dress

All Hussar regiments in 1834 wore the bell-top shako, The 15th were the only regiment to have its shako in scarlet. The body and crown were scarlet cloth, the top edged with 2 in. of regimental-pattern lace. The rosette on the front of the shako was of gold lace with a button in the centre. The boss was of gold cord with a scarlet velvet centre embroidered with the Royal cipher. The black, patent-leather peak had a border of gold embroidery and was edged with gilt brass. Gold caplines and flounders were worn. Lionhead side pieces with gilt chinchain completed the shako. The plume was of falling dark green feathers.

Uniform

The jacket was of blue cloth with 3-in. collar, edged with lace and ornamented with russia braid. It was single-breasted with 5 rows of buttons, the centre row of ball buttons and the other rows of half-ball buttons. The tunic had 19 rows of gold gimp bars across the front, ornamented with loops of russia braid. The cuffs were pointed and decorated with gold lace and russia braid. Two buttons were worn on the cuffs. The jacket was edged all round with regimental-pattern lace, terminating in two gold knobs at the back, the lace passing around the welts and side seams at the back. This lace was ornamented with russia braid. The pelisse was of scarlet cloth, with similar braiding and ornamentation to that on the jacket. Collar and cuffs were of fur, and a narrow line of the same fur was repeated around the bottom of the pelisse. Plainted necklines were attached for the wearing of the pelisse when slung from the shoulder. Overalls were in dark blue cloth with a 2-in. stripe of regimental-pattern lace down the outside seams.

Accoutrements

The waist-belt consisted of 1¼-in. gold lace backed with scarlet leather, with gilt snake fastening and three rings, from which hung the two sword slings and three sabretache slings. The sabretache was of scarlet cloth background, edged with gold lace. The design was a crown above scrolls bearing the regimental battle honours, and in the centre was a lion and crown superimposed on a trophy of arms and flags. There were two more scrolls at the base, with battle honours; the crown in the centre and the trophy of arms had a small amount of leaf embroidery on each side. The pouch was of similar design and had a gold-embroidered zigzag border. The pouch belt was of gold Austrian wave lace on a scarlet cloth background with gilt buckle slide and tip. The shabraque was of scarlet cloth edged with regimental-pattern lace, the fore part being pointed and embroidered with the crown and Royal cipher. The back was long, tapering to a point with embroidered Royal cipher and crown above the regimental device. The seat cover was made of black lambskin edged in red cloth vandyked.

Weapon

Sword. Officers carried the sword pattern 1822 with a 3-bar steel hilt, including a chequered top piece which continued into the backpiece; this was again chequered, for some 2 in. above the guard. The grip was of fish skin bound with 3 silver wires. The blade was slightly curved and was $32\frac{1}{2}$ in. from shoulder to point and $\frac{7}{8}$ in. wide at the shoulder. It was carried in a steel scabbard with top and middle rings, and the overall length of the sword was approximately 38 in.

38. 2nd Dragoon Guards. Officer, 1836

Head Dress

The helmet worn from 1834 until 1843 was a gilt helmet richly ornamented. The peak was edged in gilt strip. On either side of the helmet were scroll ornaments, and the back peak, trimmed in gilt brass, was ornamented with scrolls. The crest was ornamented on both sides with oak leaves. The front plate was a large sunray with the Royal arms pinned on. The Royal arms had the cap of maintenance. A band ran round the hat with the regimental number and name, '2nd or Queen's Dragoon Guards'. The chin scales were highly ornamented and attached to the helmet on both sides by large gilt rosettes. A bearskin crest was worn, which could be detached, and instead a crouching lion fitted on the front, as in the close-up in the illustration. This helmet gave way to a less elaborate pattern in 1843.

Uniform

A scarlet long-tailed coatee was worn. The Prussian collar 3 in. deep was black, with two gold loops at either end with regimental-pattern buttons. Gilt brass shoulder epaulettes were worn. The cuffs were round and black and ornamented with a 'V' of regimental-pattern lace with a button in the centre. The turnbacks were white kerseymere and had a button and gold embroidery at the join. A waist sash was worn, of gold, with crimson stripes similar to the light Dragoon and lancer girdle. White gauntlet gloves were worn. Dark blue overalls with a broad gold lace stripe were worn, with a broad gold lace stripe of regimental-pattern lace, and Wellington boots with spurs completed the uniform.

Accoutrements

A white buff leather crossbelt was worn in this form of dress with a black patent-leather pouch. The waist-belt was white buff with rectangular regimental-pattern buckle and with sword slings. The cloak was worn rolled across the front of the saddle, and a valise was carried on the back with the number 2 DG.

Weapon

Sword. Heavy Cavalry officers at this period carried the 1834 pattern sword, which was the first design to incorporate the honeysuckle pattern hilt. The guard was of steel, and the backpiece had 2 ears which overlapped the leather-covered wooden grip and were riveted to it. The straight blade was 35 in. long from shoulder to hatchet point and $1\frac{1}{2}$ in. wide at the shoulder. It was carried in a heavy steel scabbard with two rings for sling suspension.

39. South Salopian Yeomanry. Officer, 1842

Head Dress

The helmet worn was of white metal for officers, and polished steel for troopers and warrant officers. This imposing head dress had a white metal skull, peak and comb. The skull portion was heavily decorated with richly gilt laurel sprays on each side. The peak at the front and neck peak at the back were bound with gilt brass edging. The ornate, pointed brass chin scales, joined under the chin with lionpaws clasps, were attached to the helmet by lionheads in gilt brass. The front plate bore the Royal arms above a scroll, with the regimental designa-tion. The plate backing the design was of a sunray pattern. On the comb at the front was fixed a richly ornamented gilt crouching lion.

Uniform

A scarlet cloth coatee with blue collar and cuffs was worn. The turnbacks on the tails were of blue facing cloth joined with a small gold-embroidered device. The collar was ornamented with gold embroidery and a button of regimental pattern. The cuffs were open at the bottom and were embroidered, with buttons. The coatee was single-breasted, with eight buttons of regimental pattern. Gold lace, box epaulettes with gold tassels were worn on both shoulders. Overalls were blue with a broad and scarlet stripe. The collar was 4 in. high, and a leather stock was worn beneath it. The leading edge of the tunic front was piped in blue.

Accoutrements

A white, patent-leather crossbelt with engraved, gilt, brass buckle slide and tip was worn over the left shoulder with a black, patent-leather pouch with gilt brass regimental badge in the centre of the back. The white, patent-leather waist-belt with rectangular, gilt brass plate had two sword slings and two sabretache slings. The sabretache was of black patent leather with gilt brass crown above a gilt star, with the badge of the South Salopian Yeomanry as shown in the illustration, but in gilt brass. The shabraque was white lambskin overall, and edged in scarlet cloth vandyked.

Weapon

Sword. Officers carried the sword pattern 1822 with a 3-bar steel hilt with a chequered top piece which continued into the backpiece. This was also chequered, for some 2 in. above the guard. The grip was of fish skin bound with 3 silver wires. The blade was slightly curved and was $32\frac{1}{2}$ in. from shoulder to point and $\frac{7}{8}$ in. wide at the shoulder. It was carried in a steel scabbard with top and middle rings, and the overall length of the sword was approximately 38 in.

40. 3rd Dragoon Guards. Officer, 1844

Head Dress

The helmet at this period was of gilt brass, reminiscent of the earlier patterns but much less ornate. This helmet was worn by all Dragoon and Dragoon Guard regiments from 1843 until 1847 when a new helmet, the Albert pattern, was introduced. The skull was plain with a crest on top ornamented with scroll work. On the front of the crest was a black leather horsehair thistle-shaped brush held in a gold embroidered boss, a large, black horsehair mane was inserted behind this, falling down over the back of the helmet and to nearly the middle of the back. This helmet was very similar to the French pattern. The front plate was of sunray pattern, with the Royal coat-of-arms below, and on a band was the regimental number and title. The chin-

chain was attached to the helmet by two large gilt rosettes.

Uniform

A scarlet single-breasted coatee with a $3\frac{1}{2}$-in. Prussian collar was worn, the collar and cuffs of regimental colour. The collar was laced round with a button and loop at each end. The Dragoon Guards had 4 loops on each forearm and the same number on the skirts. The epaulettes were gold straps with a crescent, and bullion lace tassel ends were worn on both shoulders. The overalls were dark blue with a broad stripe of gold regimental-pattern lace down the outside seam. White gauntlet gloves were worn. The ankle boots were of black leather.

Accoutrements

A $2\frac{1}{4}$-in. gold lace crossbelt with gilt buckle slide and tip was worn over the left shoulder, holding in the centre of the back a morocco leather pouch box with a blue velvet flap laced round the edge and a gold embroidered Royal cipher surmounted by a crown. A waist-belt of gold lace with 2 sword slings and 3 sabretache slings was worn with a gilt rectangular buckle.

Weapon

Sword. In 1834 a new pattern of sword had been ordered for officers of Heavy Cavalry regiments. This was the first sword to incorporate a honeysuckle design in the bowl guard, which design has been copied in the patterns of 1896 and 1912. The sword had a steel guard with a leather-covered wooden grip, and steel backpiece with two ears which overlapped the grip and were riveted to it. The blade was 35 in. from shoulder to point and was parallel to within 4 in. of the hatchet point. It had a strong back and a diamond-pointed edge. The blade width was $1\frac{1}{2}$ in. It was carried in a heavy steel scabbard with a large trumpet-shaped mouthpiece and suspended from two rings 8 in. apart.

41. 3rd Light Dragoons.
Officer, 1846

Head Dress

The shako was of black beaver 7 in. deep in the front and 8 in. deep at the back. The top was 8 in. in diameter, of patent leather and sunk down about $\frac{1}{4}$ in. At the top of the shako was a band of oak-leaf lace $1\frac{3}{4}$ in. wide. The badge was a gilt and silver Maltese Cross with a crown above, with a regimental device in the centre. The borders on each crosspiece bore the battle honours. The peak was of patent leather embroidered on the front edge to the width of 1 in. The chinchain was gilt and fitted on to the helmet by ornaments of regimental pattern on which there was a running horse. The plume was of white swan feathers for officers.

Uniform

The jacket was of blue cloth with red collar and cuffs. The coat was double-breasted with 2 rows of buttons, 8 buttons in each row down the front. The turnbacks were also of red cloth with a gold bullion fringe in the centre back. There were 3 buttons of regimental pattern on each side. The cuffs and sleeve were edged in gold lace, the cuffs being ornamented by gold russia braid.

The epaulettes were plain, gold lace boards, fringed at the end $2\frac{1}{2}$ in. deep. The caplines were of gold cord with acorn cords wound twice round the shako and crossing at the back. The girdle was 3 in. wide with 2 stripes of crimson backed with red leather, fastening on the underside with leather straps and buckles and externally with gold loops and toggles. The overalls were dark blue with 2 $\frac{3}{4}$-in. gold lace stripes of regimental pattern down the outside seam of each leg with a small light between.

Accoutrements

The waist-belt was $1\frac{1}{4}$-in.-wide gold lace with snake buckle and 2 sword slings, 1 long, 1 short. In between the slings 3 1-in. sabretache slings were suspended. The sabretache was $12\frac{1}{2}$ in. deep with gold embroidered crown and V.R. in the centre above regimental device and honours. The crossbelt was 2-in.-wide gold lace with $\frac{1}{2}$-in. silk stripe and silver chains and pickers, buckle slide and tip suspending in the middle of the back, a black leather pouch box with silver flap and gilt crown and V.R. monogram in the centre.

Weapon

Sword. Officers carried the sword pattern 1822 with 3-bar steel hilt, with a chequered top piece which continued into the backpiece. This was also chequered, for some 2 in. above the guard. The grip was made of fish skin, bound with 3 silver wires. The blade was slightly curved and was $32\frac{1}{2}$ in. from shoulder to point and $\frac{7}{8}$ in. wide at the shoulder. It was carried in a steel scabbard with top and middle rings, and the overall length of the sword was approximately 38 in.

42. 1st Bengal Light Cavalry. Officer, 1846

Head Dress

The lance cap worn at this period by all regiments was much larger than the pattern worn in 1900. The top was of red cloth and was 10 in. square. The top was crossed diagonally by 2 strands of gold cord, which also went down the corners, measuring 5 in. from the top of the cap to the waist. On the left side of the top was a gold bullion rosette with the Royal cipher in velvet in the centre. The cap was very full at the waist, almost vertical. There were 2 rows of regimental lace at the base of the top. The helmet plate was of brass with silver fittings. The peak was edged in brass and there was a false peak at the back with 2 broad and 2 narrow strips of patterned lace. The chinchain and lionhead bosses were of gilt brass as was the plume holder. The helmet plate was a triangular brass plate with the badge of crossed laces decorated with foliage with a Garter in the centre and bearing the initials BLC on a black velvet background. The complete

depth of the cap was 9 in., and the whole was topped with a white swan feather plume. The caplines were of bullion cord which tied around the body once and attached to the cap.

Uniform

The jacket was of blue cloth. It was double-breasted with 2 rows of regimental pattern buttons down the front, 9 buttons in each row. All the buttons were equidistant. The last button in each row was flat, so that it lay under the gold and crimson striped girdle. The collar was of white kerseymere 3 in. deep with 2 large silver embroidered tabs on each side. The cuffs were also white with a slashed flap with 4 buttons on it, the whole edged and embroidered. There were 2 buttons at the back of the waist above the slashed flap skirts and 3 buttons on each flap, edged in silver lace. The lining and the turnbacks were of white kerseymere. The trousers were of blue cloth with a $\frac{1}{2}$-in. striped silver lace down the outer seam. The stock was of black silk. The epaulettes were of blue cloth heavily embroidered with silver lace with a silver fringe at the end, $2\frac{1}{2}$ in. deep.

Accoutrements

The pouch belt was $2\frac{3}{4}$ in. wide with a blue silk train in the centre. It was tied in blue leather and had a silver chain and pickers and buckle slide and tip. The pouch itself was a solid silver flap with a gilt badge in the centre, of BLC surmounted by a star. The sabretache was of dark blue cloth, backed with the leather pouch and edged in silver lace on the front;

crossed lances with a star appeared in the top angle and the initials BLC in the centre of the cross; below the lances there was a wreath of foliage. The shabraque had a pointed front with the Royal cipher embroidered in silver on the tail, which was also pointed. The same device appeared on the tails as did on the sabretache, with the exception that there was a scroll beneath the lances. The tips had silver hanging tassels. The shabraque was of dark blue cloth edged in regimental-pattern silver lace.

Weapon

Sword. Officers carried the sword pattern 1822 with a 3-bar steel hilt, including a chequered top piece which continued into the backpiece, and this was again chequered for some 2 in. above the guard. The grip was of fish skin bound with 3 silver wires. The blade was slightly curved, and was $32\frac{1}{2}$ in. from shoulder to point and $\frac{7}{8}$ in. wide at the shoulder. It was carried in a steel scabbard with top and middle rings, and the overall length of the sword was approximately 38 in.

43. 1st Dragoon Guards. Officer, 1847

Head Dress

The helmet worn by the 1st (or King's) Dragoon Guards was known as the Albert pattern. The helmet, in the case of Dragoon Guards, was all gilt brass, and those of the Dragoons, except the 2nd, the Scots Greys, were white metal with gilt fittings. The gilt helmet was edged on both the front and back peak with gilt brass strip and richly ornamented with gilt brass foliage. The badge was a cut metal star in silver mounted on a brass shield. In the centre in gilt brass was an oval, surrounded by a Garter with the regimental title. In the centre was the Royal monogram, VR. Large gilt rosettes fitted the chinchain on each side of the helmet. The gilt shield in the centre was surmounted by laurel and oak leaves on each side, and surmounted by a crown. On top of the helmet was a square leaf-pattern gilt plate with a plume holder made up of 2 rows of 4 or 5 ornamented leaf sockets. The plume, surmounted by a gilt rosette, was of black horsehair.

Uniform

The coatee was of scarlet cloth with blue collar and cuffs. The collar had 2 rows of lace on each end of the collar, with a gilt regimental-pattern buckle at the end. The skirts were short and squared at the ends. There were 9 buttons down the front of the coatee. The skirts of the coatee had false turnbacks with an embroidered ornament. (A button was worn but discontinued in 1837 to save expense in the last year of the reign of William IV.) The cuffs were square and ornamented in a pattern of lace with embroidered drooping ends which had a button in the centre. Gold lace epaulettes with bullion tassels were worn on each shoulder, and on these were worn the badges of rank embroidered in silver lace. On the epaulettes was a small button of regimental pattern at the neck. A crimson and gold sash was worn around the waist, with bow and tassels worn on the left front of the hip. The overalls were dark blue material with a broad gold stripe on the outside seam of both legs.

Accoutrements

A sword belt was worn under the sash with 2 wide sword slings and 3 smaller sabretache slings in gold regimental-pattern lace. The pouch belt was all gold edged in blue-velvet and on morocco leather with gilt buckle slide and tip of regimental pattern. The pouch was leather with an embroidered flap. The material was dark blue edged around and ornamented with a crown above the Royal cipher VR and with the battle honours, PENINSULA and WATERLOO. The rest of the pouch was embroidered in a gold leaf device. The sabretache was worn very long in the King's Dragoon Guards, of the same pattern as the pouch and edged in wide lace.

Weapon

Sword. Heavy Cavalry Officers at this period carried the 1834 pattern sword, which was the first design to incorporate the honeysuckle pattern hilt. The guard was of steel, and the backpiece had two ears which overlapped the leather-covered wooden grip and were riveted to it. The straight blade was 35 in. long from shoulder to hatchet point and 1½ in. wide at the shoulder. It was carried in a heavy steel scabbard with 2 rings for sling suspension.

44. Gloucester Hussars. Officer, 1847

Head Dress

The head dress at this period was of the Austrian shako shape. This came about at the time of the marriage of Lady Codrington's sister to the Austrian ambassador. Sir William Codrington was an officer in the Hussar regiment. The shako had straight sides about 10 in. in height with a row of gold lace at the top about 3 in. in width with a red train in the centre and red edging, and there were gold cords ornamenting the shako on the front. There was a large boss of gold cord with the Royal cipher VR embroidered in the centre. The peak was of black leather, the one at the back permanently turned up. The plume was of green feathers. The caplines were of gold, attached to the cap at the back, going around the neck and attaching to the front of the tunic, ending in flounders and tassels.

Uniform

The uniform was of red cloth double-breasted with 2 rows of silver buttons, 9 in each row, the last button in each row being flat to fit under the girdle, which was of gold lace with a red silk train in the centre. The collar and cuffs were of blue cloth ornamented with silver lace. There were 2 buttons at the back at waist level, and the skirts were lined in white kerseymere with a button at each point of the turnbacks. The epaulettes were of silver lace with a 2-in. fringe at the end in silver bullion. The trousers were of blue cloth with a gold stripe down the outside seam with a light in between.

Accoutrements

The sabretache was of blue face cloth with a dark blue leather backing and pocket. The front was edged in silver of a very distinctive pattern. In the centre was a very ornate V and I interwoven in gold lace, above this was the Hanoverian crown with 5 loops. This cipher had a scroll underneath, bearing the regiment's title. The pouch belt was of gold lace and the pouch was a flap in blue cloth edged in silver with the same motif as the sabretache in the centre, and was attached to the pouch belt by 2 gilt oval rings. The sheepskin was black with a red lining, and the throat plume was of red horsehair.

Weapon

Sword. Officers carried the sword pattern 1822 with a 3-bar hilt with a chequered top piece which continued into the backpiece. This was also chequered, for some 2 in. above the guard. The grip was of fish skin bound with 3 silver wires. The blade was slightly curved and was $32\frac{1}{2}$ in. from shoulder to point and $\frac{7}{8}$ in. wide at the shoulder. It was carried in a steel scabbard with top and middle rings, and the overall length of the sword was approximately 38 in.

45. Bundelkund Legion. Officer, 1847

Head Dress

This Indian Army regiment wore a large fur busby about 10 in. high with a $1\frac{1}{2}$-in. insert into the crown into which the red bag was fitted and hung down on the right-hand side. The caplines were of gold cord. The chin-chain was of gilt brass interlocking rings.

Uniform

The Alkeerak, which was a long coat with a slit up each side, was of blue cloth, the chest being heavily embroidered down to about 8 in. above the waist in gold and red lace. The fastening down the front was with hooks and eyes. The shoulders were also heavily embroidered almost down to the elbow, as were the cuffs. The shoulder and cuff embroidery were about 6 in. apart. The sides of the slits were ornamented with gold lace about 1 in. wide, and were embroidered on the front corners. The overalls were of red cloth with a gold stripe down the outside seam with a light in between.

Accoutrements

The waist-belt, sword and sabretache slings were of gold lace with a red train down the centre. The pouch belt was also of gold lace with a red train and silver buckle, slide, chains and pickers, and the pouch, in what can be gleaned from various sources, was of red cloth edged in lace with the initials BL embroidered in the centre. The sabretache was of scarlet face cloth laced all round in gold with an embroidered BL in the centre, also in gold. The saddlecloth was of leopard skin with a gold fringe around the edge. This was worn over the shabraque, which was of blue cloth edged in gold lace. The fore end and rear were rounded, and both bore the initials BL, embroidered in gold.

Weapon

Sword. Officers carried the sword pattern 1822 with a 3-bar steel hilt with a chequered top piece which continued into the backpiece; this was also chequered for some 2 in. above the guard. The grip was of fish skin bound with 3 silver wires. The blade was slightly curved and was $32\frac{1}{2}$ in. from shoulder to point and $\frac{7}{8}$ in. wide at the shoulder. It was carried in a steel scabbard with top and middle rings, and the overall length of the sword was approximately 38 in.

46. 1st Madras Light Cavalry. Officer, 1848

Head Dress

The shako was the light dragoon one, being slightly bell-shaped. It was of black beaver with a thick row of silver lace round the top, with an oak-leaf pattern. The shako plate was a large silver Maltese Cross with a crown above and the letters MLC in the centre. The caplines were plaited in the front, almost hiding the leather peak from view. On the right-hand side of the shako were flounders and tassels. The caplines then went over the left shoulder and attached on to the left side, the ends being ornamented with flounders and tassels. The chinchain was made of overlapping scales attached to the helmet by lionheads. The plume was of white swan feathers.

Uniform

The collar and cuffs were a pale buff colour. The tunic was of French grey cloth, the collar being edged all round in silver lace, and the pointed cuff being highly ornamented with lace. There were 3 rows of buttons down the front of the tunic, the centre row of ball buttons and the 2 outer rows of half-ball buttons. The complete front of the tunic was frogged with about 18 rows of silver lace. The welts and seams at the back were of silver lace ornamented with russia braid.

Accoutrements

The pouch belt was of silver lace with a buff train in the centre ornamented with silver buckle slide and tip and chains and pickers. The pouch had a silver flap with the Royal cipher with crown above in the centre. The shabraque was of French grey cloth, the front and back both being pointed, edged all round with silver lace. The front end was ornamented with 1 MLC surrounded by a laurel wreath all in silver lace. On the back end is a crown with 1 MLC in laurel wreath with 1 scroll each side. Below this is a star with 2 scrolls and foliage underneath. The whole is in silver lace.

Weapon

Sword. Officers carried the sword pattern 1822 with a 3-bar steel hilt with a chequered top piece which continued into the backpiece. This was also chequered, for some 2 in. above the guard. The grip was of fish skin bound with 3 silver wires. The blade was slightly curved and was $32\frac{1}{2}$ in. from shoulder to point and

$\frac{7}{8}$ in. wide at the shoulder. It was carried in a steel scabbard with top and middle rings, and the overall length of the sword was approximately 38 in.

47. 2nd Dragoons. Sergeant, 1854

Head Dress

The head dress at this period for the 2nd Dragoons was of black bearskin with a white plume on the right-hand side coming out from a gilt bomb, with the Royal arms and St. Andrews Cross underneath with the honour WATERLOO. On the back was a silver running horse of Hanover, almost hidden by the fur. The chinchain is of brass interlocking rings hooked on to the bearskin. The pillbox hat shown in the close-up is of blue cloth, and the top has a white button in the centre and a white zigzag line round the outer edge.

Uniform

The coatee was of scarlet cloth with blue collar and cuffs. The front had 6 buttons down the front of regimental pattern. The collar was of blue cloth with 1 gold lace tab each side on the front, with a button on each. The cuff, also of blue cloth, had a 'V' in gold lace with a button in the apex. The tails had 2 slashed flaps edged in gold cord with 3 buttons on each flap. The turnbacks were of white kerseymere. The overalls were of blue cloth with a 2-in. gold stripe down the outside seam. The bottom and inside of the legs were covered with leather. The epaulettes were brass scales with a brass crescent, and were held by a small regimental-pattern button.

Accoutrements

Two thick, white straps went over both shoulders, crossing at the front and the back. On the one going over the right shoulder was a knapsack, and on the one going over the left shoulder was a carbine swivel and hook. The gauntlet gloves were of white buff leather. The carbine belt had a black pouch affixed.

Weapons

Sword. Although a new sword was ordered in 1853 for all cavalry, issues were protracted, and Heavy Cavalry still, at this time, retained the 1830 pattern sword. It had a steel bowl guard lined with white buckskin and a wooden grip covered with leather. The blade was slightly curved and terminated in a hatchet point. It was carried in a heavy steel scabbard with two rings for sling suspension.

Carbine. In July 1836 certain regiments of cavalry were equipped with the 'Victoria' carbine, which was introduced to the service by George Lovell. This weapon was of ·733 in. calibre with a barrel 2 ft 2 in. long. It was equipped with a percussion side lock and a swivel rammer, designed so that it could not be lost while reloading on the move.

48. 4th Light Dragoons. Trooper, 1854

Head Dress

1844–55 pattern, of black beaver 7 in. deep at the front and 7 in. deep behind. The crown, of black leather, was 8 in. in diameter. The top of the shako was bound with 1-in. yellow worsted braid and bore a brass Maltese Cross plate with regimental number and title in the centre and battle honours around the outside edges of the Cross. The plate was surmounted by a Victorian crown. A white horsehair plume of 14 in. was worn, and the caplines were of yellow worsted cord. Brass chinchain and rosettes completed the head dress. The illustration shows a trooper in marching order during the Crimean War, wearing the black oilskin cover and no plume.

Uniform

The coatee was blue and double-breasted, with 2 rows of regimental-pattern buttons, with 8 in each row. Collar, cuffs and turnbacks were of scarlet facing cloth, with 2 buttons on each cuff. The skirts were plaited, with 3 buttons on each side, together with a yellow, worsted back fringe. Trousers were blue with a double yellow stripe. The girdle was made of woven yellow webbing with 2 red stripes. Brass scale epaulettes were worn, except during the Crimean War, when they were left off, leaving the brass fitments on the shoulders of the coatee exposed.

Accoutrements

Buff leather with brass fittings was used for pouch belt, waist-belt and sword slings. The former was worn over the left shoulder, and over the right shoulder was carried a white

canvas haversack and a round water-bottle of blue painted wood on a brown leather strap. The ammunition pouch was in black leather, and the carbine swivel on the pouch belt was of steel. The waist-belt under the coatee, below the girdle, had a rectangular brass plate. A small, white buff pouch on the right front contained percussion caps for the carbine.

Weapons

Sword. Although in 1853 both Light and Heavy Cavalry troopers were ordered a new pattern of sword, issue of this was delayed, and in 1854 the 4th Light Dragoons troopers were still carrying the 1829 pattern. This had a 3-bar steel hilt with the grip covered in leather and bound with wire, and with an all-steel backpiece with 2 ears which fitted around the grip and which were held to it by a rivet. It had a slightly curved blade, fullered on the back edge and terminating in a single spear point. It was carried in a heavy steel scabbard with a ring near the mouthpiece and another some 18 in. down the scabbard.

Carbine. In July 1836 certain regiments of cavalry were equipped with the 'Victoria' carbine, which was introduced to the service by Lovell. This weapon was of ·733 in. calibre, with a barrel 2 ft 2 in. long. It was equipped with a percussion side lock and a swivel rammer designed so that it could not be lost while reloading on the move.

49. 8th Hussars. Trooper, 1854

Head Dress

The brown fur busby was 9 in. deep at front and rear. The bag was of scarlet cloth, crimped at the crown inset 1½ in. below the top. Lionheads were worn at either side with brass chinchains. Caplines were of yellow cord, and the plume was of white horsehair with scarlet base, in a brass socket. (On active service this was not worn.) Oilskin covers were issued, but these do not appear to have been worn.

Uniform

The other ranks' jacket was made entirely of blue cloth, with yellow worsted cord on the collar front, back seams and cuffs. The front of the jacket had 19 rows of yellow cord with loops at the ends; there were 3 rows of buttons, the centre row being ball buttons and the other 2 rows half-ball buttons. The pelisse was made of scarlet-lined lambswool, with its bottom edge bordered in imitation lambswool. Overalls were of dark blue cloth with a broad yellow stripe down the outer seams. The barrel sash consisted of scarlet worsted cord with woven barrels and acorns.

Accoutrements

Pouch belt, waist-belt and sword slings were white buff leather, with brass fittings. The ammunition pouch was in black leather, and the carbine swivel on the pouch belt was made of steel. The pouch belt was worn over the left shoulder; over the right shoulder was carried a white canvas haversack and a round water-bottle of blue painted wood on a brown leather strap. The waist-belt was worn under the coatee, below the girdle, and bore a rectangular brass plate. A small, white buff pouch, containing percussion caps for the carbine, was worn on the right front.

Weapons

Sword. Although in 1853 both Light and Heavy Cavalry troopers were ordered a new pattern of sword, issue of this was delayed, and in 1854 the 8th Hussars were still carrying the 1829 pattern. This had a 3-bar steel hilt with the grip covered in leather and bound with wire, and an all-steel back piece with two ears which fitted around the grip and were held to it by a rivet. The blade was slightly curved, fullered on the back edge and terminating in a single spear point. It was carried in a heavy steel scabbard with a ring near the mouthpiece and another some 18 in. down the scabbard.

Carbine. In July 1836 certain regiments of cavalry were equipped with the 'Victoria' carbine, which was introduced to the service by Lovell. This weapon was of ·733 in. calibre with a barrel 2 ft 2 in. long. It was equipped with a percussion side lock and a swivel rammer designed so that it could not be lost while reloading on the move.

50. 11th Hussars. Officer, 1854

Head Dress

The busby was of brown fur 9 in. deep at front and rear. The crimson cloth bag was crimped at the crown inset 1½ in. below the top. Lionheads were worn at either side with gilt chinchains. The caplines were of gold cord. The plume, 10 in. high, was of white egret with crimson base, and had a gilt socket and ring. It was not worn in marching order. Oilskin covers were issued to the Hussars in the Crimea, but do not appear to have been worn.

Uniform

The blue cloth jacket had a 3-in. collar edged with lace and decorated with russia braid. It was single-breasted with 5 rows of buttons, the centre row being ball buttons and the other rows half-ball buttons. Nineteen rows of gold gimp barsa decorated the front of the tunic, ornamented with gold lace and russia braid. Two buttons were worn on the cuffs. The jacket was edged all round with regimental-pattern lace, terminating in 2 gold knobs at the back. This lace was ornamented by russia braid. The pelisse was of blue cloth with similar braiding and trimming to that on the jacket. Collar and cuffs were of fur, and a narrow line of the same fur was around the bottom of the pelisse. Plaited neck lines were attached for the wearing of the pelisse when slung from the shoulder. Overalls were of booted pattern and made of crimson cloth with 2 stripes of gold lace ¾ in. wide with light between. A gold and crimson barrel sash was worn at the waist, with large gold acorns at the ends.

Accoutrements

The waist-belt was 1½-in. wide gold lace, backed with scarlet leather, with gilt snake fastening and 3 rings, from which hung the 2 sword slings and the 3 sabretache slings. The sabretache was of crimson cloth background edged with 2¾-in. gold lace. The design in the centre consisted of the Royal cipher reversed, with ducal crown and scrolls above, and scrolls bearing battle honours and a metal sphinx beneath. The top scroll below the crown bore the regimental title. The pouch belt worn over the left shoulder was of gold regimental-pattern lace 1½ in. wide, with gilt buckle, slide and tip, and silver breastplate chains and pickers. The pouch box was in red leather with gilt metal flap and silver ornaments.

Weapon

Sword. Officers carried the sword pattern 1822 with 3-bar steel hilt, with a chequered top piece which continued into the backpiece. This was also chequered, for some 2 in. above the guard. The grip was made of fish skin, bound with 3 silver wires. The blade was slightly curved and was 32½ in. from shoulder to point and ⅞ in. wide at the shoulder. It was carried in a steel scabbard with top and middle rings, and the overall length of the sword was approximately 38 in.

**51. 13th Light Dragoons.
Trooper, 1854**

Head Dress

1844 pattern, of black beaver, 7 in. deep at the front and 8 in. deep at the rear. The black leather crown was 8 in. in diameter. The top of the shako was bound with 1-in. yellow worsted braid, with a brass Maltese Cross plate bearing the regimental number and title in the centre, and battle honours around the outside edges of the Cross. The plate was surmounted by a Victorian crown. A white horsehair plume of 14 in. was worn, and caplines of yellow worsted cord. Brass chinchain and rosettes completed the head dress.

Uniform

The coatee was blue and double-breasted with 2 rows of regimental-pattern buttons, 8 in each row. Collar, cuffs and turnbacks were made of white facing cloth, with 2 buttons on each cuff. The skirts were plaited, with 3 buttons on each side and a yellow worsted back fringe. The trousers were of blue cloth with a double white stripe. However, in March 1854 this cavalry regiment, together with 3 others, was issued with experimental grey overalls with double white stripes. The girdle was made of woven yellow webbing with 2 red stripes. Brass scale epaulettes were worn, except during the Crimean War, when they were left off, leaving the brass fitments on the shoulders of the coatee exposed.

Accoutrements

Pouch belt, waist-belt and sword slings were in buff leather with brass fittings. The ammunition pouch was of black leather and the carbine swivel on the pouch belt was steel. The pouch belt was worn over the left shoulder; over the right shoulder was carried a white canvas haversack and a round water-bottle of blue painted wood on a brown leather strap. The waist-belt worn under the coatee, below the girdle, had a rectangular brass plate. A small, white buff pouch, containing percussion caps for the carbine, was worn on the right front.

Weapons

Sword. Although in 1853 both Light and Heavy Cavalry troopers were ordered a new pattern of sword, issue of this was delayed, and in 1854 the 13th Light Dragoons troopers were still carrying the 1829 pattern sword. This had a 3-bar steel hilt with the grip covered in leather and bound with wire, and with an all-steel backpiece with 2 ears which fitted around the grip and were held to it by a rivet. It had a slightly curved blade, fullered on the back edge and terminating in a single spear point. It was carried in a heavy steel scabbard with a ring near the mouth-piece and another some 18 in. down the scabbard.

Carbine. In July 1836 certain regiments of cavalry were equipped with the 'Victoria' carbine, which was introduced to the service by Lovell. This weapon was of ·733 in. calibre with a barrel 2 ft 2 in. long. It was equipped with a percussion side lock and a swivel rammer designed so that it could not be lost while reloading on the move.

52. 17th Lancers. Trooper, 1854

Head Dress

The lance cap had a leather skull, with cloth sides and leather top 8¾ in. deep in front and 9 in. behind. By 1854 the height at the front was only 8 in. and the top was 8½ in. square. The square, upper part of the body was covered in white cloth with yellow worsted cord at the quarters; the top was in black leather with small, brass-ornamented corners. At the narrow part of the body was a strip of yellow worsted braid with a blue line in the centre. The peak was of black leather. A stamped brass plate bore the Royal arms above the skull and crossbones and motto 'Or Glory'. A brass lion and chinchain were worn. The black horsehair plume was carried in a brass holder on the left front of the top. A blue and yellow boss was worn below the plume holder, with a regimental button in the centre. The illustration shows a trooper in marching order, wearing the oilskin cover without the plume. The caplines, of yellow worsted cord with acorns, passed around the neck and were secured at the back of the cap.

Uniform

The dark blue, cloth coatee had white collar, cuffs and turnbacks, and sleeve welts and back seams. It had a double row of regimental-pattern buttons, 9 in each row. The skirts were plaited and 7 in. deep, being 3½ in. wide at the tail. Full dress included brass shoulder scales stamped with skull, crossed bones and lances, but was not worn during the Crimean campaign. Overalls were blue with a double white stripe, but in March 1854 the 17th Lancers were issued with experimental grey ones. The girdle was of yellow webbing with 2 scarlet stripes, as for Light Dragoons.

Accoutrements

Pouch belt, waist-belt and sword slings were in white buff leather with brass fittings. The ammunition box was in black leather. The pouch belt was worn over the left shoulder, and over the right shoulder was carried a white canvas haversack and a round water-bottle of blue painted wood on a brown leather strap. The waist-belt was worn under the coatee below the girdle, and had a rectangular brass plate. On the right front, a white buff pouch was worn, which contained percussion caps for the pistol, as the 17th Lancers were not equipped with carbines.

Weapons

Sword. Although in 1853 both Light and Heavy Cavalry were ordered a new pattern of sword, issue of this was delayed, and in 1854 the 17th Lancers troopers were still carrying the 1829 pattern sword. This had a 3-bar steel hilt with the grip covered in leather and bound with wire, and with an all-steel backpiece with 2 ears which fitted around the grip and were held to it by a rivet. It had a slightly curved blade, fullered on the back edge and terminating in a single spear point. It was carried in a heavy steel scabbard with a ring near the mouthpiece and another some 18 in. down the scabbard.

Pistol. Lancers were equipped with the pattern 1842 pistol with a 9-in. barrel of musket bore. They had a short butt and percussion side lock of musket size, and were fitted with swivel rammers so that they could be loaded on the move without the risk of dropping the ramrod.

Lance. The regiment was equipped with the lance pattern 1846, which had a 9-ft pole of male bamboo, but, due to short supply, ash was more likely to be used. The lance head had a diamond-section blade some 12 in. long and $2\frac{1}{2}$ in. at its widest, tapering to an acute point. It was held on to the shaft by 2 steel languets some 3 ft long, which continued down the pole and were secured to it by 5 screws on each side. The bottom end of the pole was equipped with a rounded shoe. At the point of balance of the lance there was a rawhide sling which went around the trooper's wrist, and at the head of the lance was flown a pennon of red-and-white bunting.

53. Royal Horse Artillery. Officer, 1855

Head Dress

In 1855 sable fur was introduced for the busby instead of the black bear-skin used previously. The busby was 9 in. deep at the front and rear and had a scarlet bag let $1\frac{1}{2}$ in. into the top. A patent-leather chinstrap was worn. The caplines, 3 in number around the body of the busby, were of gold cord. The plume was 10 in. high, of white egret with white base and had a gilt socket and ring.

Uniform

A blue cloth shell jacket, edged around the bottom front leading edge and collar in gold cord and forming a figure eight $2\frac{1}{2}$ in. deep at the base of each back seam, was worn. A scarlet collar edged in gold cord had a grenade embroidered in silver $2\frac{1}{4}$ in. at each end. On each side of the jacket there were between 15 and 18 loops of gold cord according to the height of the wearer, fastened with gilt ball buttons. At the top of the tunic on each collar-bone was an Austrian knot and curl. Gold cord piped the back seams, with a crow's foot at the top of each seam and an Austrian knot at each waist. Plaited shoulder cords were worn on each shoulder. The cuffs were heavily embroidered with figure braiding, denoting, in the illustration, a field officer. The overalls were blue with $1\frac{3}{4}$-in. strip of scarlet down the outer seams and were booted in black leather.

Accoutrements

A gold lace crossbelt 2 in. wide lined in blue morocco leather and with a buckle slide and gilt grenade encircled by a wreath as a tip. The belt suspended a pouch worn in the middle of the back. The pouch was in blue morocco leather of the collapsible type. The 6¾-in. long flap was 4⅛ in. deep, covered the blue cloth, and was edged in ¾-in. lace and embroidered with the Royal arms above an oak and laurel wreath with *Ubique* below. Below the wreath was a gun in gun-metal and below the gun was the motto *Quo fas et gloria ducunt*. The sword slings were gold lace, as were the sabretache slings. The sabretache was blue morocco leather faced in blue and edged in ½-in. lace with the same devices as the pouch.

The shabraque was edged in gold lace and was of blue cloth with a crown and VR reversed in gold embroidery on each hindquarter, beneath which was a large, gilt metal gun above a scroll bearing the word *Ubique*. The shabraque had a black lambskin seat cover edged in red cloth vandyked.

Weapon

Sword. General Orders of 1833 stated, 'On no occasion will an R.H.A. officer appear, whether in jacket, pelisse or frock coat, without his sword, which shall be regulation cavalry with a steel scabbard.' The regulation cavalry officer's sword at that time had a 3-bar hilt in steel with a slightly curved blade having a ramrod or pipe back (i.e. of circular section). The blade was 35½ in. long × 1¼ in. at the shoulder, and was carried in a steel scabbard suspended from 2 loose rings 9 in. apart. However, there was a slight difference between swords of the Royal Artillery and those of the cavalry which came in by custom rather than by

regulation. The pommel on the Light Cavalry officer's sword was rounded and chequered, whereas that of the artillery officer had a stepped pommel which was not chequered.

54. 16th Lancers. Trooper, 1855

Head Dress

The lance cap had a leather skull with a square top 8½ in. square, the sides being covered in black cloth for the 16th over a bamboo frame, quartered by yellow worsted cord and ornamented at the top with brass corners. At the slim part of the body was a strip of yellow worsted braid with red line in the centre which encompassed the cap. The peak was of black varnished leather. The helmet plate was a large, brass, triangular sunray stamped with the Royal arms and regimental device. The brass interlocking chinchain was attached to the cap by brass lionheads. The red and white horsehair plume fitted into a brass socket covered by a yellow worsted boss with red centre and regimental button. The caplines of yellow worsted cord with acorns passed around the neck and secured at the back of the cap. The black plume shown was worn in India.

Uniform

A scarlet cloth coatee adopted for all Lancers in 1830 but discontinued by the 9th, 12th and 17th in favour of blue in 1838, was worn by the 16th Lancers. It was double-breasted with blue collar and cuffs. The welts and back seams were of the same colour as the coatee. On each sleeve there was a scarlet slashed flap with 5 small buttons of regimental pattern. Unlike other Lancers at this period, there was no worsted yellow back fringe, instead there were 2 buttons at the hip and slashed flaps on the skirt with 3 buttons on each side. The Prussian collar was ornamented with 2 stripes of yellow lace terminating in a button on each at the neck. Brass scaled epaulettes were worn on each shoulder. The overalls were blue with a double scarlet stripe on the outside seam of each leg with a blue light between. The girdle was yellow webbing with 2 scarlet stripes $\frac{3}{8}$ in. wide. Gauntlet gloves of white buff leather were worn.

Accoutrements

The pouch belt, waist-belt and sword slings were in white buff leather with brass fittings. The ammunition box was in black leather. The sword belt was worn under the coatee, but visible at the front below the girdle and had a rectangular brass plate. On the right front a white buff pouch was worn containing percussion caps for the pistol, as the 16th Lancers were not equipped with carbines.

Weapons

Sword. By this date most regiments of cavalry had been issued with the cavalry trooper's sword 1853 pattern. This was the first sword that was a common issue to both Light and Heavy Cavalry. It had a heavy curved blade with a wide fuller along the back edge and terminated in a spear point. The guard was still 3 steel bars, as with the previous pattern, but the grip of this weapon was strengthened by the continuing tang at the full width of the blade up to the pommel and the riveting to it of 2 chequered leather scales. The sword was carried in a steel scabbard with 2 loose rings.

Pistol. Although a new pistol was ordered in 1856, it is likely that at this date the troops would still be carrying the pattern 1842 pistol with a 9-in. barrel. The use of pistols by cavalry had been abolished in 1838, but lancers had been permitted to retain 1 each. Other cavalry regiments were issued with sufficient pistols for warrant officers and trumpeters. This particular weapon was a percussion, musket-bore pistol designed by Lovell, with a 9-in. barrel and a swivel ramrod. One peculiarity of this weapon was that it had no butt ring for a lanyard as did other military pistols of this period, which seems to be an extraordinary omission for a weapon carried by a horseman.

55. 4th Light Dragoons. Officer, 1856

Head Dress

The shako was known as the second Albert pattern and introduced for infantry and Light Dragoons on 16 January 1855. The shako was of black beaver $5\frac{1}{2}$ in. at the front, $8\frac{3}{4}$ in. at the side and $9\frac{1}{8}$ in. less in diameter than the head size of the wearer. A patent-leather band $\frac{5}{8}$ in. wide ran around the bottom of the shako, with small buckle at the rear.

A band of 1¾-in.-diameter oak-leaf-pattern lace ran around the top. A nearly horizontal squarish peak was 2¼ in. deep with ¾-in. gold wire embroidery.

Burnished gilt chinchains were worn attached to the shako on each side by rosettes. A small gilt lion-head was fixed at the back and a gilt hook to fasten up chinchain. The gold caplines went all round the shako and fitted round the neck. A hair plume in scarlet, standing 5 in. above the shako and falling in a gilt leaf and ball socket, completed the head dress. The shako plate was a crown surmounting a Maltese Cross in gilt and silver, of regimental pattern. The shako plate shown in the illustration was the pattern in brass worn by other ranks. The battle honours were arranged around the edges of the Cross on a band and in the centre a Garter with the words 'The Queen's Own Light Dragoons' and the Roman numeral IV in the centre. The background of the Cross was dimpled.

Uniform

A blue single-breasted tunic was worn, edged all round with gold cord. The collar edged in gold cord was 2 in. high and of regimental facing, in this case scarlet. The front of the tunic had 5 bars of gold cord across the chest, terminating at each end in gold caps and drops and fastening at the breast with gold worked olivets. The cords were 8 in. at the top and 4 in. at the bottom. The cuffs were pointed and edged in gold cord in an Austrian knot. Twisted cord epaulet-tes were worn with 2 small regimental-pattern buttons. The back seams were piped in gold cord starting with a trefoil at the top, passing under a netted cap at the waist and terminating at the bottom of the skirt in a knot. The skirt was long, 9 in. in length for an officer 5 ft 9 in. in height (varying lengths of skirt were worn by officers of different heights). The overalls worn were dark blue, of the same material as the tunic, and had 2 yellow stripes down the outside seam of the leg with a light between. The overalls were booted, that is, protected, around the bottom and the inside of the leg with leather.

Accoutrements

The crossbelt was of gold lace with a central train of scarlet and backed with morocco leather with silver buckle slide and tip and chain and pickers. The pouch was leather with a silver flap with a crown and VR in gilt on it. The sword belt was worn under the tunic with gold sword slings with a scarlet train. The shabraque was blue edged in gold with regimental device embroidered on the hindquarter. The seat cover was in black lambskin.

Weapon

Sword. Officers carried the sword pattern 1822 with a 3-bar steel hilt with a chequered top piece which continued into the backpiece, also chequered for some 2 in. above the guard. The grip was of fish skin bound with 3 silver wires. The blade was slightly curved and was 32½ in. from shoulder to point and ⅞ in. wide at the shoulder. It was carried in a steel scabbard with top and middle rings, and the overall length of the sword was approximately 38 in.

56. Prince Alfred's Own Cape Town Cavalry. Officer, 1860

Head Dress

The helmet worn by the Cape Town Cavalry was the Albert pattern. The helmet was in white metal, and both the front and back peaks, which were edged in gilt brass strip, were richly ornamented in gilt brass foliage. Large rosettes were worn on either side of the helmet with a gilt brass chinchain. The badge was a cut metal star in silver, with the letters in scroll, C.T.C., on it. The star was mounted on a brass shield, surrounded by laurel and oak leaves and surmounted by a crown. On top of the helmet was a square, gilt-ornamented plate with a plume holder made up of 2 rows of 4 or 5 ornamented leaves. The plume was of white horsehair, fitted into the leaf socket.

Uniform

The jacket was a short, blue, single-breasted shell jacket of the type worn as the undress or stable jacket by British Regular Cavalry regiments. The jacket had white, face cloth collar and cuffs and was piped down the leading edge of the jacket with white. The cuffs had silver lace with a blue train edging in a pointed pattern, and the collar was edged in silver. The ranking of the officer was shown on the collar. Twisted silver epaulettes were worn on both shoulders. The tunic had 8 silver buttons of regimental pattern. The overalls were also blue with a double silver stripe with a blue light in between. Ankle boots with black and silver spurs completed the uniform.

Accoutrements

A silver lace pouch belt with silver buckle slide and tip was worn over the left shoulder, attached to an embroidered pouch on the back. The pouch of black leather had a blue velvet flap edged in silver lace with a dark blue train with, in embroidery, the crown in gold above the monogram C.T.C. with a spray of leaves below. The sabretache, of the same design in embroidery, was slung on the left hip from 3 silver lace slings with a blue train. The sword slings and belt were of the same pattern, and the belt had a small silver snake buckle. The silver and dark blue lancer pattern girdle was worn fastened underneath with a leather strap and buckle, and on top with 3 silver loops and divots. The saddlecloth was of black lambskin. The shabraque, when worn, was of blue cloth edged in white silver lace with a blue train, and it had the same ornamentation as the sabretache on it.

Weapon

Sword. Officers carried the Light Cavalry officer sword pattern of 1882. This had a hilt of 3 fluted steel bars, a chequered top and back-piece and a wooden grip covered in fish skin. It was bound with 3 strands of silver wire. The blade was slightly curved and terminated in a double spear point. It was embossed on one side with the Royal coat-of-arms, and it was usual for the obverse side to carry the regimental badge. The sword was carried in a nickel-plated steel scabbard with a ring at the mouthpiece and another some 8 in. below for sling suspension.

Historical Note

The Cape Town Cavalry was one of the 4 Cape regiments to be honoured by Prince Alfred on his South Africa visit of 1860. The regiment was raised in 1857 and disbanded in 1889. The regiment acted as a bodyguard for ceremonial occasions.

57. 17th Lancers. Officer, 1865

Head Dress

The top of the cap was of white cloth 7¼ in. square. The top was crossed diagonally by gold cord, which also went down the side angles. At the waist of the cap was a band of gold lace with a train of blue silk in the centre. The triangular sunray plate on the front was of brass with the Royal arms, skull and crossed bones and battle honours pinned on in silver. The peak was of black leather with 2 rows of gold pearl embroidered on the edge. The cap-lines were of gold lace attached to the rear of the cap, going round the body twice and looping up on the left side ending in gold acorns.

Uniform

The tunic was of blue cloth with a white collar edged in gold lace and a pointed cuff edge measuring 6 in. It had 2 rows of buttons, 9 in each row. The last one in each row being flat so that it fitted under the gold-and-red striped girdle. The lapels buttoned back on the fourth button, giving the tunic a white front. The slashed flap skirts of the tunic were edged in gold cord, with 3 buttons on each flap. The welts and back seams were piped in white. The booted overalls were of blue cloth lined on the inside leg and round the ankle in black leather. A double white stripe went down the outside seam with a light in the centre. No epaulettes were worn, as the ranking in this period was on the collar.

Accoutrements

The pouch belt was of gold lace with a ½-in. train of white silk in the centre. The buckle slide and tip and chains and pickers were in silver. The pouch was a silver flap bearing the crown and Royal cipher in gilt brass in the centre. The sword and sabretache slings were of gold lace of regimental pattern. The sabretache was of black patent leather with the skull and crossed bones in the centre. Both ends of the shabraque were rounded, edged all round with gold lace with a blue light in the centre. The front end was embroidered with the crown and V.R. in gold lace. The back was of crossed lances with the skull and crossed bones and the scroll bearing the words 'Or Glory' below. The skull and bones were in silver lace, the rest in gold. Above this was a crown and below the lances were the letter and numbers 17L, all in gold lace.

Weapon

Sword. Officers carried the sword pattern 1822 with a 3-bar steel hilt with a chequered top piece which continued into the backpiece; this was also chequered, for some 2 in. above the guard. The grip was of fish skin bound with 3 silver wires. The blade was slightly curved and was $32\frac{1}{2}$ in. from shoulder to point and $\frac{7}{8}$ in. wide at the shoulder. It was carried in a steel scabbard with top and middle rings, and the overall length of the sword was approximately 38 in.

58. Taplow Lancers. Officer, 1870

Head Dress

The lance cap had a black leather skull with cloth sides $6\frac{1}{2}$ in. deep in the front and $8\frac{1}{2}$ in. at the back. The rectangular upper part of the badge was covered in red cloth, top and sides being quartered by gold cords and the corners being ornamented in brass. At the narrow part of the body there was a strip of gold lace with a blue line running through the centre. The peak was of black leather bound round the edge in gilt brass. A stamped sunray plate on which were mounted the Royal arms with the scroll underneath bearing the words 'Taplow Lancers' in silver. A brass chinchain attached to the cap by

brass lionheads was worn. The plume was of white swan feathers and carried in a gilt brass holder on the left top side. A gold lace boss was worn below the plume holder, with a blue velvet patch in the centre bearing the Royal cipher in gold lace. The caplines were all gold cord with acorn ends which went round the neck, around the body once and were secured at the back of the cap.

Uniform

Normal lancer pattern tunic of red cloth with a blue butterfly front which was obtained by turning the left side back on to itself, thus exposing the blue. Two rows of buttons in the front and 7 buttons in each row 8 in. apart at the top and 4 in. apart at the waist, the last button in each row being flat to go under the girdle. The collar and cuffs were ornamented with 1-in. regimental-pattern lace, the cuff being $8\frac{1}{2}$ in. in length from top to bottom with 2 buttons on each cuff. The collar and cuff were of blue cloth. The girdle was of gold lace $2\frac{1}{2}$ in. wide with 2 blue stripes fastening with gold loops and olivets on the right side. The overalls were of blue cloth with 2 red stripes down the outside seam with a light in the centre. Tunic had blue welts and seams. Rank was shown on the collar.

Accoutrements

The crossbelt was 2 in. wide with a $\frac{1}{4}$-in. red silk stripe in the centre lined in red leather with silver breast ornament, pickers, and chains, buckle tip and slide of regimental pattern.

The pouch was a silver flap $7\frac{1}{2}$ in. long $2\frac{3}{4}$ in. deep with the Royal cipher in gilt in the centre, with a red leather box on the back. The sword belt was worn under the tunic with gold lace sword slings with a red centre stripe. White buff leather gauntlets.

The shabraque had rounded corners on the front and back, edged in gold lace 2 in. wide, on the front the Royal cipher and crown, on the tail crossed lances with S.B.Y.C., one in each angle with crown above. The crest was in gold, but the lance pennants were red and white, the holster covers were black lambskin with red vandyked edge.

Weapon

Sword. Officers carried the sword pattern 1822 with a 3-bar steel hilt with a chequered top piece which continued into the backpiece; this was also chequered for some 2 in. above the guard. The grip was of fish skin bound with 3 silver wires. The blade was slightly curved and was $32\frac{1}{2}$ in. from shoulder to point, and $\frac{7}{8}$ in. wide at the shoulder. It was carried in a steel scabbard with top and middle rings, and the overall length of the sword was approximately 38 in.

59. Canterbury Yeomanry Cavalry. Trooper, 1875

Head Dress

The helmet worn by the Canterbury Yeomanry Cavalry of New Zealand, who were raised in 1864, was a peculiar black felt helmet following the general lines and shape of the leather helmet used by some British mounted infantry regiments of Yeomanry and the Guernsey Militia at a slightly earlier period. The helmet was similar in style to the Russian infantry helmet of the Crimean period, and was about to be adopted by British infantry on the outbreak of the Crimean War. All supplies in store were then issued to volunteers. The Canterbury Yeomanry copied their style. The helmet was edged in silver with a silver band above the peak and with a chin scale fitted each side under a rosette. The back had a centre rib in silver, and a cruciform top held a plume holder in silver and a red falling horsehair plume. On the front of the helmet in silver were the letters C.Y.C.

Uniform

A scarlet coat of infantry pattern with blue collar and cuffs. The cuffs were ornamented in blue braid with a knot above the cuff. The leading edge and all round the bottom was piped in blue. The tunic had 7 buttons and no shoulder cords of any kind. The lace was allowed to be gold for officers because of a certain sergeant-major who had served in the 8th Hussars and who was sergeant-major of the Yeomanry. The breeches were of blue cloth with a double red stripe down the outside seam. Butcher boots and steel spurs completed the uniform.

Accoutrements

The crossbelt worn by the regiment was in black leather with silver chain and pickers. The pouch was also in black leather. The sword belt worn beneath the coat was black leather with black leather sword slings, 1 long and 1 short. The saddlecloth was plain, and black lambswool was worn as shown in the illustration.

Weapon

Sword. The sword with which this regiment was equipped was the 1864 pattern cavalry trooper's weapon. It had a sheet steel hand guard 4 in. wide, pierced through the front face with 4 triangles in the shape of a Maltese Cross. Two slots at the back of the guard were used for the sword sling, and the grip was 2 leather sides riveted to the tang. The blade was 35 in. from shoulder to point and slightly curved, terminating in a double spear point. It was carried in a steel scabbard with rings for sling suspension.

60. 1st Dragoon Guards. Officer, 1879

Head Dress

The helmet was of cork covered in white doeskin, with 6 seams down the sides. The peak measured 3 in. in the front, 2 in. at the side and 4 in. at the back. A white 6-layer pugri was worn round the helmet. The chin-chain was of gilt brass.

Uniform

Tunic was of scarlet cloth with blue collar and cuffs. The cuff was edged in gold lace with the ranking on both sides. The cuffs were pointed and ornamented with an Austrian knot in gold lace. The tunic had 6 buttons down the front, and the leading edge was piped in blue. The back had 2 buttons at the waist and slashed skirts, each flap ornamented with 3 buttons and edged in gold cord. The breeches were of blue cloth, with a wide gold stripe down the outside seam. The insides of the legs were covered in leather.

Accoutrements

The crossbelt and pouch were of white and went under a red twisted cord on the left shoulder. The waist-belt was white with a regimental-pattern buckle in the centre and a brown leather holster on the right-hand side. The white haversack and the water-bottle were slung from the right shoulder and hung down on the left side.

Weapons

Sword. Officers carried the Heavy Cavalry officer's sword pattern of 1856. This had a scroll hilt in steel with a chequered top and backpiece and a fish skin grip bound with 3 silver wires. The blade was 35 in. from shoulder to point, $1\frac{1}{2}$ in. wide at the shoulder, slightly curved and terminated in a double spear point. Some regiments had their own regimental badge interwoven with the scrolls on the face of the guard.

Revolver. The Government Enfield revolver carried by officers at this period was designated the pistol revolver breech-loading Enfield Mark I ·476 calibre. This was the British Government issue weapon to officers, designed by Owen Jones at the Royal Small Arms factory at Enfield Lock, Middlesex. It replaced the ·450 Adams revolver and had a chamber carrying 6 cartridges, was double-action, and the barrel was released for reloading by operating a lever with the right thumb. This revolver was the most powerful man-stopper in the world at this time.

61. 11th Hussars. Trooper, 1881

Head Dress

A busby in black sealskin or racoon $7\frac{3}{4}$ in. high was worn. A cherry red or crimson bag, hung down the right-hand side, was set $1\frac{1}{2}$ in. into the top. The bag was edged in yellow russia braid with centre stripe, terminating in a yellow cord boss at the base of the bag. A yellow corded boss on the top front of the busby hid a brass plume holder, in which was carried a white on crimson horsehair plume with brass ring in a brass flame socket. Yellow caplines of 2 rows encircled the busby. Brass chinchain backed with black leather completed the head dress.

Uniform

A blue cloth tunic edged all around, as was the collar, with yellow worsted cord, was worn. The tunic had on each side 6 loops of yellow cord with bosses and drops of the same. The back seams were piped with yellow cord, and 3 eyes at the top passed under a yellow boss at the waist, ending in an Austrian knot which reached to the bottom of the skirt.

An Austrian knot of yellow cord was worn on each cuff. On the shoulder were 2 rows of yellow cord with brass buttons. The tunic was fastened by hooks and large plain brass ball buttons. The yellow caplines ended in plaited acorns hooked on the right breast. Crimson breeches with 2 yellow stripes divided by crimson piping, together with black butcher boots and steel spurs, completed the uniform.

Accoutrements

A white buff crossbelt with brass buckle, slide and tip and black leather pouch were worn over the left shoulder. In marching order, as shown, a white canvas haversack was carried over the right shoulder. A valise with '11.H' in yellow was carried behind the saddle. The oval metal mess tin was strapped to this. The Oliver pattern water-bottle hung down the right side, from under the valise. A carbine bucket was carried also on this side. The sword was carried on the saddle on the other side. The cape was worn rolled over the front of the saddle.

Weapons

Sword. Troopers carried the 1864 pattern sword. This had a sheet steel hand guard some 4 in. wide, pierced in the front with 4 triangles in the shape of a Maltese Cross, and there were 2 slots at the back of the guard for the sword knot. The tang was the full width of the grip, which consisted of 2 chequered leather scales, secured to the tang with 5 iron rivets. The overall length of the sword was 41 in., and the blade, which was slightly curved, was 35 in. from shoulder to point. It was carried in a heavy steel scabbard with rings at the mouthpiece, and a third of the way down the scabbard.

Carbine. This regiment carried the Martini Henry carbine, which was adopted by the British Government in April 1871. It had a 22-in. barrel, and the charge used was 70 grains in a coiled brass case, or 65 grains in a solid case. The first pattern had a bore of ·450 and used the Boxer cartridge; in the later pattern the bore was reduced to ·303. It remained in service until the early years of the twentieth century, when the decision was taken to adopt a magazine weapon.

62. 2nd Dragoons. Sergeant, 1882

Head Dress

A bearskin cap like those of the Foot Guard regiments was worn by other ranks of the 2nd Dragoons, a white cut feather plume originating from a brass grenade plume holder on the left side. The plume came up the side to the middle of the top, and the plume holder was round with flames from the top. The design portrayed in our illustration shows the Royal arms over St. Andrew and cross above the scroll, with the battle honour WATERLOO. A silver running horse of Hanover was worn at the rear of the head dress half-way up, and is normally missed, as partially obscured by the fur. A brass chin-chain, backed with black leather, was worn.

Uniform

A scarlet tunic, with blue collar and cuffs, was worn. The collar was piped with yellow worsted cord, and the cuffs were ornamented with yellow, worsted cord Austrian knots. The skirts were pleated and piped with yellow cord and had 3 buttons of regimental pattern. The tunic's leading edge was piped with blue, and had 7 buttons down the front. Blue breeches with a broad yellow stripe were worn, with black leather butcher boots and steel spurs. The gloves were white, buff gauntlets.

Accoutrements

The waist-belt was of white buff with brass fittings and snake fastening. Two buff sword slings hung from the left side. On the right front of the belt an infantry pattern ammunition pouch was worn in marching order. A white buff crossbelt and a black leather pouch were worn over the left shoulder. In marching order, a white canvas haversack on a white canvas strap was carried over the right shoulder, with an 1875 Oliver pattern water-bottle on a brown leather strap. A metal, round mess tin was carried on the right back of the saddle and a lambskin over the greatcoat at the front. Also on the right rear of the saddle a carbine bucket was attached.

Weapons

Sword. Cavalry at this period carried the 1882 pattern trooper's sword.

This was in reality the 1864 sword which had been modified by lapping the edges of the guard, making it stronger, but of course narrower. Also, the sword knot slot was removed from the top to the bottom of the guard, and the bottom of the guard was also raised above the pommel, forming a hand-stop. Two lengths of blade were available, the 1882 pattern (long), which was 35⅜ in., and the 1882 pattern (short), which was 33 in.

Pistol. The carbine that was carried was the Martini Henry. It was adopted by the British Government in April 1871, and it had a 22-in. barrel. The charge used was 70 grains in a coiled brass case, or 65 grains in a solid case, the first pattern having a bore of ·450 and using the Boxer cartridge. In the later pattern the bore was reduced to ·303. It remained in service until the early years of the twentieth century, when the decision was taken to adopt a magazine weapon.

63. Camel Detachment. Trooper, 1884

Head Dress

A white pattern sun helmet, introduced for all troops on foreign service in 1877, was worn. The helmet was cork covered in 6 panels of white duck and crowned with a zinc top covered in white duck which screwed into an 8-bar collet. A white linen pugri was worn tied around the helmet. Brass chin scales

were attached at either side of the helmet, on hooks.

Uniform

A newly introduced foreign service uniform in grey was worn with 2 patch pockets on the breast and done up with 5 brass buttons. Plain grey shoulder tabs were done up with a small brass button at the neck. Plain pointed cuffs and stand collar completed the tunic. The breeches were of bedford cord in a light brown sandy colour. Dark blue puttees and brown boots completed the uniform. The uniform was the first attempt at a special uniform for foreign active service which did not employ scarlet.

Accoutrements

Blue-lensed goggles were issued to the men against sun glare and sand, and when not in use were worn as illustrated. A brown leather bandolier of single round, with flaps, was worn over the left shoulder, while a haversack and water-bottle of the Oliver pattern were worn over the right shoulder. A white buff waistbelt with brass fittings and universal pattern brass socket was worn with a white, buff infantry pattern ammunition pouch on the right side. A bayonet frog was worn on the belt on the left hip.

Weapons

Rifle. The weapon carried by other ranks was the Martini Henry rifle, which was adopted by the British Army in 1871. This was a breech loading rifle which fired the Boxer cartridge of ·450. The breech was operated by lowering a lever below the breech, which dropped a breech block allowing the cartridge to be inserted manually into the barrel. The lever was then returned, sealing off the cartridge, which was then fired by a pin in the breech block actuated by the trigger. The barrel was 33 in. long and the weight of the rifle was 8 lb 10 oz.

Bayonet. For use with the above rifle, the Enfield pattern bayonet of 1856 was specially converted by bushing the ring to fit the Martini Henry barrel.

64. Royal Horse Guards. Drummer, 1887

Head Dress

The peaked cap or jockey cap as it was known was of dark blue velvet, domed, with a button on the top. The peak was about 2 in. deep and very square.

Uniform

The knee-length coat was made from royal maroon cloth and was braided entirely with regimental-pattern lace. It had a stand collar and wing epaulettes. The lace on the coat had gaps in between to let the maroon show through, which gave the uniform a very regal appearance. On the front and back was a large crown and Royal cipher. In all, cipher and crown measured about 18 in., and they were embroidered on a separate piece of maroon cloth so that when the reigning monarch died the cipher could be easily changed. The breeches

were of white buckskin and the high winged jackboots of black leather. Polished steel spurs were worn.

Accoutrements

Two silver kettle drums were carried on the horse, one each side. On each, drum banners were carried. The drum banners were of patterned material embroidered all around with foliage. In the centre was the complete Royal coat-of-arms with supporters surmounted by a crown, with the Royal cipher VR. The saddle-cloth was of crimson cloth and was a rear housing only. The back edges were rounded and edged in a broad band of regimental-pattern lace. On each side of the back was the Royal crown with lion above over the Garter star surrounded below and on each side with leaf ornaments with battle honours interwoven among the leaves. Leather patches were sown each side at the bottom to prevent the boots of the drummer rubbing the saddle cloth. A black throat plume was attached to the harness under the horse's head. The reins of the horse were attached to the stirrup irons to leave the hand free.

65. 10th Hussars. Officer, 1888

Head Dress

The busby was of brown sable fur $6\frac{1}{4}$ in. high in the front and $7\frac{3}{4}$ in. at the rear. A 2-in. deep, oval gold, gimp cockade was worn on the front at the top. A scarlet cloth bag was set into the top and fell down on the right-hand side. This bag was edged in gold lace, as was the centre seam. A white, ostrich feather plume, 15 in. high was worn. The base was black vulture plumes. The plume holder was a gilt ball with 5 leaves on the top. The chinchain was of gilt brass corded chain linked together lined in black leather. The caplines were of gold cord, hooked on to the busby under the bag, passed diagonally across the body 3 times and then hooked up on the left side. The cords had acorn ends.

Uniform

The tunic was of blue cloth. Across the front of the tunic were 6 pieces of lace ending in caps and drops, fastening down the front with gimp lace olivets. On the back seams, a double line of gold gimp lace, forming an Austrian knot at the top then going on down the seam under a gold netted button and then ending in an Austrian knot. The heading and bottom edge were laced all round in gold gimp lace. The collar was edged in ¾-in. gold lace. The cuff was ornamented with an Austrian knot in gold gimp lace. The illustration shows a field officer where the collar and cuff were very highly ornamented with extra lace. The shoulder cords were of plaited chain gimp lace and the trousers of blue cloth with two ¾-in. gold lace stripes with a light in between.

Accoutrements

The crossbelt was of black patent leather with gilt chain ornaments. The pouch also, of black patent leather with a gilt ornament in the centre of regimental pattern. The sabretache was faced in scarlet cloth backed with red morocco leather. The front was edged in regimental pattern lace. In the centre was the Royal cipher VR in gold lace with a small X underneath. Under this were 5 scrolls bearing battle honours. Above the VR cipher were the Prince of Wales' feathers in silver lace with a crown embroidered over the feathers. Under this were 2 scrolls bearing the motto 'Ich Dien'. The shabraque was of scarlet cloth. The front end was slightly pointed, with the Royal cipher embroidered in gold lace. The back end was pointed, embroidered with a crown and Prince of Wales' feathers with the number 10 in Roman numerals. Underneath this, a scroll with an H underneath. The whole was edged with 2 rows of regimental lace, with a light in the centre. The horse furniture was of black leather decorated with cowrie shells.

Weapon

Sword. Officers carried the sword pattern 1822 with a 3-bar steel hilt with a chequered top piece which continued into the backpiece; this was also chequered, for some 2 in. above the guard. The grip was of fish skin bound with 3 silver wires. The blade was slightly curved and was 32½ in. from shoulder to point and ⅞ in. wide at the shoulder. It was carried in a steel scabbard with top and middle rings, and the overall length of the sword was approximately 38 in.

66. 2nd Life Guards. Farrier, 1890

Head Dress

A white metal helmet was worn not only by the troopers but also by farriers of the Life Guards and the Royal Horse Guards. The helmet was of the same basic pattern as that worn by Dragoon Regiments (except the 2nd), and had a pointed peak edged all around with brass trim, the back peak also being trimmed in the same way. Across the helmet above the peak was brass ornamentation, laurel on the left and oak leaves on the right. A broad strap of oak-leaf-patterned brass ran down the back seam from the top to the brass trimming. The badge was a large oval with white metal Garter star in the centre, the oval being encircled with the collar of the Order of the Garter and with a St. George badge hanging from the centre. The whole badge was surrounded by a wreath of oak and laurel leaves and surmounted by the crown of the reigning monarch. The top of the helmet had a rayed plate in which fitted the plume holder, a white metal holder in a brass ball. The plume in the case of the farriers was black. The chin-chains were brass interlocking chain backed with leather and attached to the helmet on each side with brass rosettes.

Uniform

The uniform worn by farriers of all regiments was blue with dark blue collar, excepting warrant officers, who had scarlet facings. The collar and cuffs were edged in gold lace. The cuffs had a 'V' of gold lace with a button in the centre, and were of gauntlet pattern, edged in gold lace. The leading edge was piped up. On the skirts were slashing corresponding to rank. In the Life Guards gold cord epaulettes were worn on both shoulders with a single epaulette from the left shoulder hooking up on a button on the tunic. No cuirasses were worn. The skirt of the tunic was piped and had 10 buttons of regimental pattern. The breeches were of white buckskin. Black jackboots with steel spurs were worn, and white gauntlets.

Accoutrements

A white buff crossbelt with blue flask cord was worn, but wider than that worn by all other ranks. At the back was a 'holster' in which to carry the farrier's axe in lieu of a pouch. A white buff waist-belt was worn with brass plate of regimental pattern, with 2 sword slings, 1 short and 1 long. The lambskin seat cover was white, edged in dark blue vandyked material.

Weapons

Sword. There were 2 patterns of Household Cavalry troopers' sword, designated the 1882 pattern long and the 1882 pattern short. Both of these had a sheet steel hand guard, pierced and decorated and incorporating the letters HC under the crown. The long pattern had a blade slightly curved $34\frac{1}{2}$ in. long, and the short had a blade $32\frac{1}{2}$ in. long. The significance of the 2 patterns was that the band carried the short and other troopers the long. This difference was discontinued in 1892.

Axe. Farriers also carried a large axe at this period, only for ceremonial decoration, but originally designed for administering the 'coup de grace' to any horse too severely wounded to be saved.

67. Governor-General's Bodyguard (Canada). Trooper, 1890

Head Dress

A white metal, cavalry pattern helmet was worn by all ranks. The helmet was bound, round the pointed front peak and the back peak, with brass trim. Across the front and around to the side was a band of laurel wreaths, and at the back running from the top of the helmet to the bottom of the back peak was a band of oak-leaf-pattern brass strip. The helmet was topped with a brass cruciform, in which was fitted the plume holder. The plume was white horsehair topped with a brass rosette. The badge was the arms of Canada on a gilt star. On both sides was a brass rosette, under which fitted the interlocking brass chinchain backed with leather.

Uniform

The uniform was of the British cavalry pattern and in fact very similar to that of the 6th Dragoon Guards, being blue. The collar and cuffs were faced with white and the shoulder tabs also were white. The front leading edge was piped in white. The buttons were brass, of regimental pattern. The cuffs were ornamented with Austrian knots and the back skirts were ornamented with heavy cavalry pattern skirt ornaments, with brass buttons. The breeches were blue with two white stripes down the outside seam of each leg with a light between. Black butcher boots and steel spurs completed the uniform.

Accoutrements

A white buff waist belt with brass buckle slide and tip was worn over the left shoulder, with black leather pouch attached to it and worn in the middle of the back. A white buff sword belt with brass snake fastening and 2 short slings were worn.

Weapons

Sword. The sword that was carried by troopers was the cavalry pattern of 1882. This was a derivation of the 1864 pattern and had a sheet steel handguard with lapped edges and with a Maltese Cross pierced out of the leading face. The slot for the sword knot was placed at the bottom of the guard. The blade was slightly curved and terminated in a spear point, and the tang was taken up through the guard to its full width and was then fitted with chequered leather scales to form the grip. The sword was carried in a scabbard of 18 S.W.G. steel with 2 rings at the mouthpiece.

Carbine. The Snider carbine had a breech-loading mechanism designed by Jacob Snider of New York. This had a hinged block which swung to one side and allowed the brass centre-fire cartridge to be inserted. It had a bore of ·573 in. and, having a length of 3 ft 4½ in., it had the unusually heavy weight of 7 lb 7 oz.

68. Shropshire Yeomanry. Trooper, 1892

Head Dress

In February 1872 a meeting was held by the officers of the Shropshire Yeomanry to consider the adoption of a new uniform for the combined South Salopian Yeomanry and the North Salopian Yeomanry. The helmet they chose was made of white metal, bound around the edge with polished brass. At each side there was a large polished brass rosette, under which was located the brass chinchain, backed on leather. The badge was a polished brass crown, below which was a cut, silver faceted star on to which was mounted a polished brass shield containing the arms of Shropshire, 3 leopards heads. On top of the helmet was a crossed brass fitting on to which a brass plume stem was fitted. A white over red horsehair plume, hanging down to the back rim of the helmet, was mounted in the holder. The plume was capped by a brass rosette.

Uniform

The tunic is of blue, dragoon pattern, with scarlet collar and cuffs. This pattern of tunic was adopted in 1882; prior to this, a blue, double-breasted tunic with red butterfly front was worn. The yellow webbing girdle with 2 red stripes was now replaced by a white, buff sword belt. The new tunic had 7 brass buttons of regimental pattern, and the leading edge was piped in scarlet. The skirts were similar to the pattern worn by the Royal Horse Guards. Officers' tunic skirts were like those of the Corporal of Horse in the Royal Horse Guards. The pointed cuffs had yellow lace edging. White gauntlet gloves were worn. The breeches were blue, with a wide scarlet stripe. Black, leather butcher boots were worn, with steel spurs.

Accoutrements

A white buff sword belt and sword slings with brass snake fastening were worn. Over the left shoulder was a white, buff crossbelt with brass buckle, slide and tip, and a black leather ammunition pouch containing carbine ammunition. The sabretache was plain black leather. The shabraque was of black lambskin with scarlet cloth vandyked border. A brown leather carbine bucket was worn on the right rear of the saddle.

Weapons

Sword. The 1885 cavalry sword was derived from the 1864 sword; this had a bowl guard with piercings at the front which resembled a Maltese Cross, and thus gave their name to the Maltese Cross hilt.

In 1882 the edges of the guard were lapped down to strengthen it and the slot for the sword knot had been placed at the bottom of the guard; a hand-stop had been fitted inside to make it more comfortable to hold.

The construction of the hilt was that the blade was continued through the guard to its full width, and 2 chequered leather scales were riveted to it, forming a comfortable and practical grip which added to the strength of the weapon. The blade was slightly curved and terminated in a double spear point. It was carried in a heavy steel scabbard with 2 rings, 1 each side of the mouthpiece, which allowed the sword to be strapped up on to the saddle.

Carbine. The carbine carried at this time was the Martini Henry. It was adopted by the British Government in April 1871, and it had a 22-in. barrel. The charge used was 70 grains in a coiled brass case, or 65 grains in a solid case, the first pattern having a bore of ·450 in. and using the Boxer cartridge. In the later pattern the bore was reduced to ·303 in. It remained in service until the early years of the twentieth century, when the decision was taken to adopt a magazine weapon.

69. Gloucester Hussars. Trooper, 1896

Head Dress

This busby was made of racoon skin and was $7\frac{3}{4}$ in. high. On the top there was a lip 1 in. deep, into which the plain red bag fitted. The bag hung down on the right-hand side. The plume was $3\frac{1}{2}$ in. high, of white on red horsehair. The chinchain was of interlocking brass links on a black leather backing and hooked into the busby. The caplines were of yellow worsted cord and fitted to a hook on the busby under the bag. They went around the neck and hooked upon the left side, ending in acorn ends.

Uniform

The shell jacket was similar to that worn in 1856 by Hussar regiments. It was of blue cloth with blue collar and cuffs. On the front there were 17 rows of yellow worsted cord with a row of 17 ball buttons in the centre and a row of flat buttons on each side at the ends of the cords. The bottom edge of the tunic was edged in yellow cord, and so were the back seams, starting with an Austrian knot at the shoulder and ending in worsted knobs. The collar was of blue cloth edged top and bottom with yellow braid, and the cuffs were ornaments with an Austrian knot. The shoulder cords were of yellow worsted. The trousers were of blue cloth with a double yellow stripe down the outside seam with a light in between. In this particular regiment the blue was a special colour known as Beaufort blue, which is a shade lighter than navy blue.

Accoutrements

The sword belt was of white webbing and worn under the jacket. Attached to it were the sword slings in white leather, which were, in turn, attached to a black leather sabretache which had the badge of the regiment in brass on the front. The crossbelt was of white leather attached to a black leather pouch with the regimental badge on the flap.

Note: The badge shown is the post-1901 pattern.

Weapon

Sword. The sword carried was the cavalry pattern of 1890. This was a further modification of the 1882 sword, which itself resulted from a modification of the 1864 sword. It had a sheet steel handguard with a Maltese Cross pierced out of the front face. The slightly curved blade was $34\frac{1}{2}$ in. from shoulder to point, and a prolongation of the blade passing through the guard with 2 chequered leather sides riveted to it formed the grip. The scabbard was of steel with rings either side of the mouthpiece.

70. 18th Hussars. Trooper, 1899

Head Dress

A busby in black sealskin $7\frac{3}{4}$ in. high was worn with a garter blue bag hanging down on the right-hand side $1\frac{1}{2}$ in. into the top of the busby. The bag was edged in yellow russia braid with a centre strip. A yellow cord boss was placed at the bottom of the bag on the braid line where the centre line met the edging. A yellow wound cord boss was placed at the top front of the busby, the top in line with the top of the busby. Behind this was the brass plume socket holding a white or scarlet horsehair plume with a brass ring and brass corded ball with leaves acting as a plume holder. Two rows of yellow worsted cord encircled the cap fastening on a ring under the bag to the right side. Brass chinchain, backed on black leather attached by a ring and hook, completed the head dress.

Uniform

A blue cloth tunic edged all around with yellow worsted cord was worn. The tunic had 6 loops of yellow worsted lace on each side, with bosses and drops at each end. The centre was buttoned, with brass ball buttons on loops of yellow cord. Yellow cord Austrian knots were worn on each cuff. The back seams were piped with yellow cord, and 3 eyes at the top passed under a yellow boss at the waist, ending in Austrian knot at the bottom of the skirt. On the shoulder were worsted cord epaulettes. Yellow caplines ending in acorns hooked on the right breast and around the neck, attaching to the busby under the blue bag at the right side. Blue overalls with double yellow stripes with a blue light between were worn together with black butcher boots and steel spurs.

Accoutrements

A white buff crossbelt and pouch were worn. A white buff sword belt with 2 sword slings hanging on the left hip was worn. On horseback the sword was attached to the saddle as shown. The cloak was worn rolled over the front of the saddle.

Weapon

Sword. The sword carried by cavalry troopers at this period was the 1899 pattern. This was one of the swords ordered as a result of the deliberations of the War Office Committee on cavalry swords. There were 2 different marks of this weapon, although both were identical. One was the sword cavalry pattern 1899, and the other was the sword cavalry pattern 1899 (converted from sword cavalry pattern 1890). These had a sheet steel hand guard with the inner edge heavily lapped to give added strength. Around the point of entry of the tang was a large cast steel mullet which also gave added strength. The tang was a continuation of the blade, $6\frac{3}{4}$ in. long, to which were riveted chequered leather scales. The blade was slightly curved $33\frac{1}{2}$ in. long and $1\frac{1}{4}$ in. wide at the shoulder, tapering to $1\frac{1}{8}$ in. at a distance of $2\frac{1}{2}$ in. from the shoulder and then remaining parallel to within 6 in. of the double spear point. It was carried in a steel scabbard with 2 fixed rings at the mouth.

71. Victoria Mounted Rifles. Officer, 1899

Head Dress

'Wide-awake' hat in buff or khaki drab was worn with a twisted cord pugri. The hat was worn turned up on the right-hand side and pinned by a regimental badge. A chinstrap was fitted, but as shown was tucked inside the hat crown. The hat was the typical hat worn by colonial and dominion troops, which reflected their role as 'rough riders' in the desolate parts of the Empire. This type of hat gave more protection from the sun than the helmet, and still survives today as worn by the Canadian 'mounties' and the Australian forces.

Uniform

The tunic was of a drab colour with purple collar and cuffs. The collar was high and edged in gold cord. The cuffs were ornamented in gold. The tunic had 5 buttons of regimental pattern. There were 2 patch pockets on the chest with small buttons of regimental pattern. Twisted gold shoulder cords were worn with the ranking of officer shown. The breeches were of bedford cord material, suitably reinforced on the inside of the leg with leather and of a drab colour. Black cavalry pattern boots completed the uniform.

Accoutrements

A brown leather Sam Browne belt with one shoulder brace running from left front over the right shoulder was worn, with 2 sword slings in brown leather pouch with regimental-pattern device. Silver chain and pickers were worn on the belt.

Weapons

Sword. Officers carried the Rifle Regiment pattern sword. This had a nickel-plated steel hilt showing 3 bars with, inset in the outward bars, a cartouche bearing the badge of bugle horn stringed surmounted by a crown. The blade was straight and of dumb-bell pattern, i.e. its cross-section was like a dumb-bell and it had no edges. It was carried in a Sam Browne scabbard.

Rifle. The rifle carried was a magazine Lee Metford Mark I, which weighed 9 lb 8 oz. It had a 30 in. barrel bored to take the ·303 cartridge, and the rifling was of 7 grooves. The magazine was a sheet steel box design to hold 8 cartridges, and the action was operated by a bolt. The nose cap of the rifle was fitted with a bar for the attachment of a sword bayonet, issued to other ranks in place of the sword for officers. It was carried in a leather boot attached to the rear of the saddle.

72. New South Wales Lancers. Trooper, 1900

Head Dress

The Australian bush hat in drab felt was worn by all ranks of the New South Wales Lancers with a red pugri encircling the base of the crown. The left side was turned up and held in position by the regimental badge, which consisted of crossed lances with an elephant's head encircled by a laurel wreath in the centre and a scroll underneath bearing the regiment's title. A dark green feather plume was attached behind the turned-up side. The caplines were white worsted cord. They fitted around the neck, encircled the body once and attached on to the left side.

Uniform

The tunic was of drab cloth, double-breasted, with collar, cuffs and plastron of scarlet cloth. The cuffs were pointed and measured 6 in. from the point of the edge of the cuff. The plastron had 2 rows of buttons, 7 in each row, of regimental pattern. The

last button in each row was flat to fit under the girdle. There were 2 buttons at the waist behind, above the two 3-pointed slashed flaps, which were edged in scarlet cord and had 3 buttons on each flap. All welts and side seams were piped in scarlet. The shoulder cords were of twisted red worsted cord. The breeches were also of drab cloth with a single red stripe down the outside seam. Brown boots and brown gloves were worn. The girdle was of yellow worsted cloth with 2 red stripes at equal distances.

Accoutrements

In mounted order a white crossbelt and pouch were worn, as well as a brown leather belt and sword frog. (In certain orders of dress, brown leather gauntlets were worn.)

Weapons

Sword. The sword carried depended on what was available for issue, and was probably the 1885 pattern. This had a sheet steel guard with a Maltese Cross piercing in the front. The edges of the guard were under to give added strength, and a slot for the sword knot was at the bottom of the guard near the handstop. The slightly curved blade, which was $34\frac{1}{2}$ in. long, protruded up through the guard to form a wide tang to which there were riveted 2 chequered leather scales to form the grip. It was carried in a steel scabbard with 2 fixed rings, 1 each side of the mouthpiece. However, if supplies had been available there was the possibility that the 1890 pattern might have been carried; this was an identical weapon except that the blade weight was increased from 1 lb 7 oz to 1 lb 9 oz.

Lance. This regiment carried the lance pattern of 1868, which had a forged head of triangular section with concave faces and a heavy, forged steel butt. It was carried with a male bamboo staff, the overall length of the weapon being 9 ft. On occasions when male bamboo was difficult to obtain an ash pole was substituted for it. At the point of balance it was equipped with a raw-hide sling, and the head was dressed with red-and-white pennons. On the march it was carried with the butt in a leather boot attached to the right stirrup iron, and the sling was positioned about the right arm.

73. 6th Dragoon Guards. Trooper, 1901

Head Dress

This helmet was in brass bound round the edge. At the top there was a crosspiece base and a plume socket 4 in. high. There was a laurel-leaf pattern round the helmet above the front peak, and an oak leaf up the back seam. The chinchain was of interlocking brass rings and fastened to the helmet by 2 rosette ornaments on either side. The 6th Dragoon Guards had a plainray star in white metal with Garter belt in centre with motto *Honi soit qui mal y pense* around it in brass and the number 6 in the centre in silver metal. The plume was of white horsehair.

Uniform

The tunic was of blue cloth with white collar and cuffs. The tunic had 8 buttons of regimental pattern, the leading edge and base of tunic being piped in white. The cuff was ornamented with an Austrian knot which was in yellow worsted cord. There were 2 buttons at the waist above the 3-pointed slashed flap at the back. Each flap was edged in yellow worsted cord and had 3 buttons on each. The trousers were also of blue cloth with a double white stripe down the outside seam with a light in the centre. The shoulder cords were of twisted yellow cord.

Accoutrements

The waist-belt was of white buff leather with a brass buckle according to regimental custom. The close-up shows an officer's undress sabretache. The front, in black leather, was $11\frac{1}{2}$ in. high and $10\frac{1}{4}$ in. wide at the widest part. In the centre was the large regimental badge in gilt brass which consisted of a Garter belt with the motto *Honi soit qui mal y pense*, with a crown above, 2 crossed carbines behind and the scroll bearing the word 'Carabiniers' upon it. The back of the sabretache consisted of a small leather pocket $8\frac{3}{4}$ in. high and $6\frac{3}{4}$ in. wide. On the top edge there were 3 gilt rings which attached to the sabretache slings.

Weapon

Sword. The sword carried was perhaps the worst designed sword ever to be put into service with the

British Army. This was the 1899 pattern. It had a hand guard in 17 gauge sheet steel with the inner edge lapped to give added strength and a large steel mullet around the point of entry to the tang. The grip, which was the major fault in the sword, was $6\frac{3}{8}$ in. long and slightly tapered from bowl to pommel, which caused the hand to slide down as a blow was struck. The slightly curved blade was $33\frac{1}{2}$ in. long and $1\frac{1}{4}$ in. wide at the shoulder, and it tapered to a double spear point. It was carried in a steel scabbard with a fixed ring both sides of the mouthpiece, the total weight of the sword and scabbard being 4 lb 13 oz.

74. 6th Dragoons. Sergeant, 1901

Head Dress

White metal helmet bound round the edge with brass tipping. At the top a brass crosspiece with a plume socket measuring 4 in. high from top to base. Above the pointed peak there was a laurel wreath and also an oak-leaf pattern up the back seam, both in brass. On the front a brass sunray star, in the centre a white metal Garter with the words *Honi soit qui mal y pense* in the centre on a black background with the number 6 in the centre. The chinchain was of brass interlocking rings fixed to the helmet by 2 brass rosettes. A white horsehair plume was worn from the spike and fell as far as the back of the helmet. A brass rosette was screwed to the top of the plume.

Uniform

Scarlet cloth tunic with the collar, cuffs and leading edge on the front edged in yellow cord. The cuff was ornamented with an Austrian knot. The tunic had 8 buttons down the front, of regimental pattern. At the back of the tunic there were 2 buttons at the waist just below the white buff waist-belt. The epaulettes were scarlet, trimmed in yellow with regimental title. The slashed flaps were dark blue with a double yellow stripe down the outside seam with a light in between. The boots were knee length in black leather.

Accoutrements

A white buff waist-belt with a snake fastening and sword slings were worn. White buff gloves were worn.

Weapon

Sword. The sword carried by cavalry troopers at this period was the 1899 pattern. This was one of the swords ordered as a result of the deliberations of the War Office Committee on cavalry swords. There were 2 different marks of this weapon, although both were identical. One was the sword cavalry pattern 1899 and the other was the sword cavalry pattern 1899 (converted from sword cavalry pattern 1890). These had a sheet steel hand guard with the inner edge heavily lapped to give added strength. Around the point of entry of the tang was a large cast steel mullet, which also gave added strength. The tang was a continuation of the blade, $6\frac{3}{4}$ in. long, to which were riveted chequered leather scales. The blade was slightly curved, 33½ in. long and 1¼ in. wide at the shoulder, tapering to 1⅛ in. at a distance of 2½ in. from the shoulder and then remaining parallel to within 6 in. of the double spear point. It was carried in a steel scabbard with 2 fixed rings at the mouth.

75. 16th Lancers. Trooper, 1901

Head Dress

The cap had a black leather body, the top having cloth sides, the whole cap being 6½ in. high in the front and 8½ in. at the top. The rectangular upper part had black cloth sides, with yellow cord at each corner. The top was black patent leather, the corners ornamented with brass leaves. At the narrow part of the body was a strip of yellow lace with a ¼-in. band of red running through the middle. The peak of the cap was of black leather. A triangular sunray plate had the Royal arms and regimental honours all stamped out in brass. The plume was of black horsehair. A yellow worsted boss with a red worsted centre, surmounted by a regimental-pattern button, was worn below the plume holder. The plume holder was of a brass flame design. The caplines were of yellow worsted cord with acorn ends, which encircled the neck, also encircled the body once and then secured to the back of the cap.

Uniform

The uniform was scarlet (the only lancer regiment to have this colour) with dark blue collar, cuff and plastron with 8 buttons of regimental pattern. The black skirts were piped in scarlet with 3 buttons each side and 2 at the waist. The centre vent seam was piped also in scarlet, as were the back seam welts and back seam sleeve welts. A crimson and yellow girdle was worn. The overalls were dark blue with a double yellow stripe down each outer seam. Twisted, yellow cord shoulder straps were worn fastened at the neck by a small brass button of regimental pattern. White buff gauntlets and black butcher boots with steel spurs completed the uniform.

Weapons

Sword. The sword carried was the 1899 pattern. This had a sheet steel hand guard lapped on the inner edge to give added strength, and a large steel mullet was fixed around the point of entry of the tang. The grip was a continuation of the blade with 2 leather sides riveted to it, and was 6½ in. long, this being the main reason why the sword was heartily disliked, as the hand slipped up and down. The blade was 33½ in. long, slightly curved, 1¼ in. wide at the shoulder and tapered to a double spear point. The scabbard was of steel with a trumpet-shaped mouthpiece and rings on each side of the mouth for attaching to the saddle or belt.

Lance. Troopers carried the lance pattern of 1868. The regulation for this lance called for a male bamboo pole with forged steel triangular head and a forged steel butt, but at times the difficulty of getting male bamboo caused contractors to fall back on ash poles. At the point of the lance, red-and-white pennons were flown, and at the point of balance there was a fixed rawhide sling. The butt of the lance was carried in a leather bucket fixed to the right-hand stirrup iron. The lance was discontinued in 1903 except for ceremonial purposes.

76. Imperial Yeomanry.
Trooper, 1901

Head Dress

The regulation slouch hat issued for the South African War of 1899–1902 was worn with the front turned up. The question of how the hat was worn seemed to have been a matter for the individual and governed by the circumstances in which it was worn. The hat was a buff khaki felt with a leather hat band in brown. No badge appears to have been worn, although pictures do show the hat turned up on the left side and held with a regimental badge. (Last stand of 17th Lancers at Magersfontein by R. Caton Woodville.)

Uniform

The tunic was the standard issue khaki serge with stand collar and 2 hip pockets with flaps but no buttons. The front was done up with 5 brass buttons. The tunic shoulder tabs fastened by a small brass button. There was no ornamented cuff on the tunic, but just a plain turned-up edge. The breeches were of bluish-grey and were cut to the pattern worn by civilians of the

time. Khaki puttees tied from the top and boots with spurs completed the outfit. The uniform of the Imperial Yeomanry of necessity became varied owing to the long treks, and the regulation issues from the Ordnance were not available in the far-flung areas. No badges, shoulder titles or pugris were worn. The uniform illustrated is fairly uniform; in fact, at some point the uniform became completely un-uniform (reminiscent of the Army in the North African desert in the Second World War).

Accoutrements

Two leather-bound bandoliers were worn, one over each shoulder. On the trek one of these was usually slung around the horse's neck. No bayonet was worn, but usually a few men carried one for use as a hunting knife. A haversack and water-bottle were worn by the rider on the trek, normally over the left shoulder, the bandolier being worn over the right. The rifle was slung in a rifle bucket worn long, and a sling around the arm supported the rifle. It is interesting to note that later the butt was worn higher to stop the rider using the rifle as a rest, and thus giving the horse a sore back.

Weapons

Rifle. Other ranks were equipped with the Lee Enfield magazine rifle Mark I. This was a weapon of ·303 calibre, the length overall being 4 ft $1\frac{1}{2}$ in. It was equipped with a magazine which held 10 cartridges, and the weapon was sighted to fire up to 1,800 yd on its leaf sight with an additional long-range sight up to 2,800 yd, but its normal maximum was 500 yd.

Bayonet. The bayonet carried with this rifle was the sword bayonet pattern 1888 Mark II, which had a double-edged blade 12 in. long, and the bayonet was fitted to the rifle with a catch on the pommel engaging in a bar on the nose cap of the rifle and a ring on the crosspiece fitting over the end of the barrel. It was carried in a leather scabbard with steel top and bottom mounts. The top mount was fitted with a stud for frog suspension.

77. Bethune's Mounted Infantry. Officer, 1901

Head Dress

Bethune's Mounted Infantry, formed by Lt.-Col. E. C. Bethune in 1900, was equipped as all mounted infantry of the period. The regulation issue slouch or 'wide-awake' hat, as it was called, was worn. It was turned up on the left side and pinned with a regimental-pattern badge. In a lot of cases the method of wearing the hat depended on the individual. A leather chinstrap was worn on the hat, fastened under the chin. The slouch hat was not only issued to Imperial Yeomanry regiments but Regular Cavalry regiments as well.

Uniform

The tunic was the standard issue khaki foreign service dress issued to all cavalry regiments. It had a stand collar and 2 patch pockets on the breast. It was single-breasted and had brass buttons of universal pattern. The breeches were of the same material and cut like civilian-pattern breeches. The puttees were issue pattern of dark green. The whole uniform was naturally subjected to small and sometimes major alterations and deviations from the pattern laid down; this was due to the unavailability of replacement clothing for outlying districts and to the harsh treatment received on active service. Brown boots and spurs were worn.

Accoutrements

A Sam Browne belt with brace over the right shoulder was worn complete with ammunition pouch. A peculiarity of the Yeomanry of specially raised units was their independence in the choice of weapons. The Mauser pistol was carried in the belt on the right hip. On the horse a blanket rolled on the front and spare shoes were carried. Mess tins of cavalry pattern, water-bottle and haversack were carried on the right side, plus any provender necessary for the horse in sparsely vegetated areas.

Weapon

Pistol. Officers carried the Mauser pistol. This was a weapon of 7·63 mm calibre and fired a very powerful cartridge with almost the same velocity as a rifle. It had a 10-shot magazine and could be fired single shot or semi-automatic. It was carried in a wooden holster which was in the shape of a shoulder stock, and this holster could be slotted on to the grip of the pistol and used in the manner of a carbine. It was of German manufacture.

78. 21st Lancers. Trooper, 1904

Head Dress

This regiment changed from Hussars to Lancers in 1896, and became the Empress of India's in 1897 after their great charge at the Battle of Omdurman. The helmet at this period was the normal lancer pattern with a black patent-leather skull $6\frac{1}{2}$ in. in front and $9\frac{1}{2}$ in. at the back. The rectangular waisted top having French grey sides with a patent-leather top with yellow cords up each corner and each corner ornamented with brass leaves. At the narrow part of the body was a strip of yellow worsted lace. The peak was of black leather. A triangular sunray plate had the Royal arms under which was a scroll bearing the regimental title. In the angle of the 2 scrolls there was the 1 battle honour KHARTOUM. The whole plate was stamped, unlike the officer's, where the arms and honour were silver mounted. The chinchain was of brass interlocking rings and attached to the cap by brass lionheads. The plume was of white horsehair. The boss was yellow worsted with a French grey worsted centre which bore the regimental button. This was worn below the plume holder, which

was of a flame design. The caplines were yellow cord with acorn ends, which went around the neck, encircled the body once and then secured at the back of the cap.

Uniform

The tunic was dark blue with French grey collar plastron and cuffs. The plastron was edged in regimental-pattern brass buttons. The back skirt was piped in French grey each side, with 3 buttons and a centre seam piping of the same colour with 2 buttons at the waist. The back seams and welts on the sleeve were also piped in French grey. Two small buttons were sewn on each sleeve above the cuff. Eight buttons were worn each side on the plastron. A crimson-and-yellow girdle was worn. The overalls and breeches were dark blue with double French grey stripes on the outside seam. On the tunic, French grey shoulder tabs were worn with metal badge (the only lancer regiment to do so). White buff gauntlet gloves were worn. Black butcher boots and spurs completed the uniform.

Weapons

Sword. The sword carried was the 1899 pattern. This had a sheet steel hand guard lapped on the inner edge to give added strength and a large steel mullet was fixed around the point of entry of the tang. The grip was a continuation of the blade with 2 leather sides riveted to it, and was $6\frac{1}{2}$ in. long, this being the main reason why the sword was heartily disliked, as the hand slipped up and down. The blade was 33½ in. long, slightly curved, 1¼ in. wide at the shoulder and tapered to a double spear point. The scabbard was of steel with a trumpet-shaped mouthpiece and rings on either side of the mouth for attaching to the saddle or belt.

Lance. Troopers carried the lance pattern of 1868. The regulation for this lance called for a male bamboo pole with a forged steel triangular head and a forged steel butt, but at times the difficulty of getting male bamboo caused contractors to fall back on ash poles. At the point of the lance, red-and-white pennons were flown, and at the point of balance there was a fixed rawhide sling. The butt of the lance was carried in a leather bucket fixed to the right-hand stirrup iron. The lance was discontinued in 1903 except for ceremonial purposes.

79. Royal Artillery Mounted Band. Drummer, 1905

Head Dress

A black busby 7¾ in. high and made of seal or raccoon skin was worn by the mounted band. A scarlet cloth bag, set into the top 1½ in., hung down on the right side to the line of the base of the busby, and was rounded at the bottom. No caplines around the busby or the neck were worn by the Royal Artillery, only the Royal Horse Artillery wore them. A brass grenade with flame was worn on the front of the busby at the top with a

red horsehair plume, unlike the rest of the Artillery, whose grenade was worn at the left side with white horsehair plume. The design of the grenade was the Royal coat-of-arms above a gun, and the Royal Artillery motto *Ubique* in one scroll and *Quo facet gloria ducunt* in 2 other scrolls. A brass chinchain was worn.

Uniform

A blue tunic with 7 brass buttons of Royal Artillery pattern, having a gun surmounted by a crown, had red collar and cuffs. The collar was piped in yellow worsted cord, and both cuffs had Austrian knots of yellow cord. The bottom of the skirt and the leading edge of the tunic were piped in yellow cord. The skirts at the back were pleated and piped in yellow cord with 3 regimental-pattern buttons on either side. The tunic had double yellow shoulder cords. Blue breeches with a 2¼-in. scarlet stripe, black leather butcher boots and steel spurs completed the uniform.

Accoutrements

The crossbelt was of white buff, with brass buckle slide and tip, and white buff pouch. A brass gun was worn on the pouch. The girdle was crimson. A blue shabraque edged in regimental-pattern lace bore the crown, Royal cipher and motto, embroidered on either hindquarter with a large brass gun under the Royal cipher and above the motto *Ubique.* Kettledrums on each side had panniers of blue cloth edged with regimental-pattern lace and with large embroidered full coat-of-arms above the gun and regimental mottoes. The horses' reins were attached to both stirrups, thus leaving the hands free.

80. King's Colonials (The King's Overseas Dominion Regiment). Officer, 1908

Head Dress

'Wide-awake' pattern buff felt hat, with a red hat band, was worn. The left side was turned up.

Uniform

The tunic was of drab cloth with 5 buttons down the front. There were no pockets on this pattern tunic. This tunic had a stand collar with 2 ¾ in. stripes going around the collar. The cuff was pointed and piped in red. It measured 6 in. from the point to the edge of the cuff. The cuff was ornamented with 5 vertical stripes ¾ in. wide in red cloth. This tunic had double vents at the back. The overalls were also of drab cloth with 2 red stripes down the outside seam with a light in the centre. The caplines were of red cloth and went round the neck, encircled the body and hooked up on the left breast. The epaulettes were of linked chain with a red backing.

Accoutrements

The crossbelt was of brown leather with lionhead chains and whistle, with the badge KC and Prince of Wales' feathers above, with a scroll below bearing the motto *Regi ad sumus coloni*. The pouch was also of brown leather, bearing the badge KC

with feathers, but with no scroll. All the fittings were brass. The girdle was of yellow worsted with 2 red stripes in the centre. The button shown in the close-up was of the 1910 pattern, when the regiment was changed to King Edward's Horse.

Weapon

Sword. Officers carried the 1896 pattern cavalry sword, which was the second cavalry sword which had the hilt decorated with the honeysuckle design. The length of the sword overall was 3 ft 5 in., and the blade 2 ft $11\frac{1}{16}$ in. It was slightly curved and tapered gradually from shoulder to point and was fullered on both sides to within 1 in. of the point. It was carried in a steel scabbard with 2 rings for sling suspension and the total weight complete with scabbard was 3 lb 5 oz.

81. 25th Cavalry. Camel Sowar, 1908

Head Dress

The head dress was a red turban with bars of dark stripes and worn over a red kulla which was a quilted pointed cap worn inside the turban.

Uniform

The sowars wore a dark green kurta with a red collar and green cuffs with red pointed edge. The front of the kurta had a line of red over the buttonholes from neck to waist with red welts each side with green in between. The front edge of the kurta from the waist was piped in red.

Shoulder chains were worn on each shoulder with regimental title in brass. The back seams and welts were piped in red. A red cummerbund was worn around the waist, tied on the left hip and the ends hanging down on the right hip with bars of dark blue. White breeches were worn with dark green puttees, and brown boots completed the uniform.

Accoutrements

A brown leather waist-belt was worn over the red cummerbund with regimental-pattern buckle with one brace from front left over the right shoulder. Sword slings were worn on the left side. The camel shabraque was green edged in a wide band of red and pointed at the rear. The numerals 25 in the centre were sewn on both hind-quarters of the shabraque. A green seat cloth was worn.

Weapon

Sword. The Indian trooper's pattern of sword was carried. This had a 3-bar hilt in steel with a wooden grip covered in brown leather and a steel backpiece with 2 ears protruding around the grip. The blade was curved and $32\frac{1}{2}$ in. from shoulder to point, nearly parallel and terminating in a hatchet point. It was carried in a black leather scabbard with steel mounts.

History Note

Originally the 5th Punjab Cavalry, and became 25th Cavalry Frontier Force in 1903. Sowar was the rank of trooper.

82. Glamorgan Yeomanry. Officer, 1909

Head Dress

A white sunhelmet of cork was covered in 6 panels of white doeskin. A white linen pugree was worn and a brass chinchain was fixed each side on to a hook and worn under the lower lip. A brass spike and dome top was fixed to the top of the helmet by a screw thread into a collet in the top of the helmet.

Uniform

A shell jacket of blue was worn with white collar and cuffs edged in gold lace and a buttoned-up white plastron with 8 buttons each side in gilt of regimental pattern. Twisted, gold cord shoulder cords were attached at the shoulders, and on these was shown the ranking. A gold-and-crimson lancer-pattern waist girdle was worn. The overalls depicted in the illustration are dark blue with a double white cloth stripe.

Accoutrements

A white, japanned leather crossbelt with black leather pouch was worn with gilt chain and pickers and buckle slide and tip. A canvas sword belt was worn under the girdle with white, japanned leather sword slings.

Weapon

Sword. Officers carried the 1896 pattern cavalry sword, which was the second cavalry sword which had the hilt decorated with the honeysuckle design. The length of the sword overall was 3 ft 5 in., the blade being 2 ft $11\frac{1}{16}$ in. It was slightly curved, tapered gradually from shoulder to point and was fullered on both sides to within 11 in. of the point. It was carried in a steel scabbard with 2 rings for sling suspension, and the total weight complete with scabbard was 3 lb 5 oz.

83. Skinner's Horse. Sowar, 1909

Head Dress

A lungi or pugree was worn in yellow cloth and had black-and-red stripes going diagonally across the front. The lungi was worn round a kulla, a small pointed cap.

Uniform

A kurta in yellow cloth was worn with a black collar and a black pointed cuff. The collar and cuff were edged in red braid. Down the front was a 2-in. band of black cloth edged in red which was the backing for the buttons. Two patch flap pockets, 1 on each side. The waist sash was of black cloth. The epaulettes were of linked chain, and the welts and back seams were piped in black. The trousers were of white cloth and worn with black puttees.

Accoutrements

The waist-belt was of brown leather with a square buckle of regimental pattern. This was worn over the cummerbund with the regimental badge in the centre of the pouch.

Weapons

Sword. The sword carried was the Indian Cavalry trooper's pattern with

a 3-bar hilt in steel, leather-covered wooden grip and slightly curved blade $32\frac{1}{2}$ in. from shoulder to point, $1\frac{1}{2}$ in. wide at the shoulder and parallel to its hatchet point. The scabbard was black leather with steel mounts and 2 rings for sling suspension.

Lance. Troopers carried the Indian pattern lance, which had a shorter and smaller head than the British pattern, and the butt was what was known as ball pattern, in that it had a large ball and a short spike at the bottom. The staff was in male bamboo and the head dressed with red-and-white pennons; at the point of balance was a rawhide sling. The lance was carried with the butt in a leather bucket attached to the right-hand stirrup iron.

84. 14th (Murray's Jats) Lancers. Risaldar Major, 1909

Head Dress

The turban was wound on the head in 2 halves with an ornate gold fringing on the left front and hanging down. The main colour of the turban was red with gold-wire embroidery. No kulla was worn in Murray's Jats.

Uniform

The kurta was dark blue with a centre line of red down the front edged in gold lace and pointed at the waist. This was ornamented with elaborate gold russia braid in a circular design outside the edges of the lace. An

Austrian knot in gold was worn on the cuff, also ornamented with the same design tracing in gold as worn on the front of the kurta. The skirt of the kurta was heavily embroidered with gold loop tracing, and was edged in red. The welts and back seams were also edged in red. The shoulder straps were peculiar to the regiment, being heavily embroidered on the shoulder and coming to an end beyond the shoulder and on the top of the upper arm in fine embroidery. The badges of rank were worn on those straps. A Kashmir cummerbund was worn, over which was placed the sword belt. The breeches were white cloth, and black boots and steel spurs completed the uniform. White gauntlets were worn.

Accoutrements

A gold lace crossbelt on red morocco leather was worn with no chain and pickers and had a red train in the centre. The waist-belt had a gilt rectangular buckle of regimental pattern with the letters MJL with XIV above, in silver. Two sword slings were worn, 1 long and 1 short, to carry the sword, which was in a steel scabbard.

Weapon

Sword. The Indian trooper's pattern of sword was carried. This had a 3-bar hilt in steel with a wooden grip covered in brown leather and a steel backpiece with 2 ears protruding around the grip. The blade was curved and 32½ in. from shoulder to point, nearly parallel and terminating in a hatchet point. It was carried in a

black leather scabbard with steel mounts.

History Note

The 14th Lancers amalgamated with the 15th Lancers in 1921 and were renamed the 20th Lancers in 1922. Risaldar major was the equivalent of the rank of major.

85. 29th Deccan Horse. Risaldar, 1910

Head Dress

A green lungi was worn tied around the head with the kulla, a pointed cap, being worn inside. The stripes on the lungi were of gold and blue.

Uniform

The kurta was of green cloth with 5 regimental-pattern buttons down the front. The kurta had a slit up both sides to just below the waist. The shoulders were protected by shoulder chains in white metal. The breeches were of white melton cloth, worn with dark blue-grey puttees and brown boots. The collar of the kurta was edged in gold lace and the cuffs ornamented in gold lace.

Accoutrements

A plain red cummerbund was worn at the waist. A gold lace sword belt and regimental-pattern buckle over this. Two sword slings in gold lace were worn attached to the sword on 2 rings at the mouth of the scabbard. A gold crossbelt and pouch were worn with silver buckle slide and tip and chain and pickers, also a black leather pouch with silver flap and gilt ornament of regimental pattern.

Note: Risaldar was the rank of lieutenant.

Weapon

Sword. Officers of this regiment carried the cavalry trooper's sword, Indian pattern, introduced in about 1860. This had a 3-bar hilt, a leather-covered wooden grip bound with 3 strands of steel wire, and the backpiece was plain. The blade was slightly curved 32½ in. from shoulder to point and parallel to a width of 1½ in. wide from shoulder to within 4 in. of the hatchet point. Depending upon the regiment, the scabbard of leather with 3 steel mounts could be either of donkey skin or camel skin.

86. City of London Yeomanry (Rough Riders). Officer, 1912

Head Dress

This helmet was the regulation pattern lance cap 6½ in. high in the front and 8½ in. high at the back. The skull was of patent leather, the back edge having 2 thin rows of lace. The rectangular top was of French grey cloth, with gold gimp and orris lace across the top and down the side angles. On the left side in front was a gold bullion boss with the Royal cipher in gold on a purple background; at the back of the boss, a socket to hold the plume stem. The plume was of French grey swan feathers. At the waist of the cap was a 1-in.-wide band of gold lace with 2 rows of gold lace below. The gilt brass sunray plate was of usual pattern, but instead of the Royal arms, the arms of the City of London were displayed in silver. The chin-chain was ¾-in.-wide burnished brass which affixed to the cap by means of lionheads. The caplines were of gold gimp and orris lace with olive ends encircling the cap once, passing around the body and looping up on the left side. The plume holder was 5 gilt brass leaves in a bomb-shape.

Uniform

The tunic was of French grey cloth with collar, cuffs and plastron of purple. The cuffs were pointed and both collar and cuffs were ornamented with gold lace, ½ in. around the collar and 1 in. around the cuff. From the point of the cuff to the edge measured 6 in. The purple plastron had 2 rows of buttons, 7 in each row. The rows were 8 in. apart at the top and 4 in. apart at the waist. The last button in each row was flat to go under the girdle. There were 2 buttons at the waist behind, above the 3-pointed slashed back, which was edged in gold cord and had 3 buttons on each flap. The welts and back seams are in purple. The shoulder cords are of gold twisted cord lined in purple facing cloth. The overalls are in French grey cloth with a double purple stripe down the outside seam with a light in the centre. The girdle is of gold lace 2½ in. wide with 2 purple silk stripes. It fastens with a strap and buckle on the inside, and gold loops and olivets on the outside. In winter a cloak was worn, of French grey cloth with purple collar and lining.

Accoutrements

The sword belt was worn under the tunic with 2 gold lace sword slings attached to it. Both slings had a purple silk train in the centre and a gilt lionhead slide at the tip. The cross-belt was of gold lace with silver chain and pickers and buckle slide and tip. The pouch was a silver flap 7½ in. long and 2¾ in. deep with a gilt Royal cipher in the centre. The box behind the flap was of wood, covered in blue leather. The gauntlets were of white buff leather.

Weapon

Sword. The sword carried was the cavalry officer's 1896 pattern. This was the second honeysuckle hilt that was adopted for cavalry officers, the first being the 1834 pattern for Heavy Cavalry. The sword was approved for wear on 11 September 1896. The blade was 2 ft $11\frac{1}{16}$ in. long from shoulder to point, was slightly curved and tapered gradually for its full length. It was fullered on both sides to within 11 in. of the point. The grip was of fish skin bound with 3 strands of silver wire, and the backpiece was of steel chequered for its entire length. It was carried in a steel scabbard with 2 rings 8 in. apart for suspension from sword slings.

History Note

The Rough Riders were formed in March 1900 to combat the strike-and-run tactics of the Boers in South Africa.

87. Oxford Hussars. Officer, 1914

Head Dress

The illustration shows the forage cap in khaki cloth 9½ in. across the crown, and the depth from the flat top to the hat band was 1¾ in. deep, but not stiffened at all in front as the latter-day forage caps were. The peak was set into the front at an angle of 45 degrees and was 1¾ in. deep in the centre. On the hat band was the badge of the Oxford Hussars, which was the AR cipher reversed with crown above and scroll and motto below. The cap had a brown leather chinstrap buttoned on each side of the peak with regimental-pattern buttons. The chinstrap was worn up and was adjustable.

Uniform

The service dress was of drab material, single-breasted and cut like a normal suit jacket to the waist, fitted at the waist like a hunting jacket, in that the skirts flared out. The skirts were approximately 13 in. long, but there was a slight variation, depending on the height of the wearer. The collar was a step collar 3 in. deep at the opening. There were 2 breast pockets with flap held down by a button, one each side of the collar measuring 6½ in. wide and 7½ in. deep. In the centre of each pocket was a box pleat. The tunic had 5 regimental buttons down the front. The cuffs were rounded and had a 3-pointed flat edged with ½-in. chevron lace. Chevron lace was also worn around the cuff, according to rank. In this case on the flap the ranking would be 3 worsted pips, as the illustration shows a captain, and there were 2 rows of chevron lace encircling the cuff. The breeches were of drab cloth to match the jacket. They were cut full at the hips and tight at the knees. They did up at the bottom with a buckle and strap or buttons. There were 2 pockets at the side. The skirt was of khaki and always worn with service dress.

Accoutrements

The belt worn with service dress was known as the 'Sam Browne'. It was made of brown leather 2⅛ in. wide and a length to suit the wearer. It had a brass buckle with double teeth and two brass 'D's for the shoulder. The cross strap was about 28 in. long. On the right side of the waist-belt the binocular pouch was fitted, and on the right the holster. On the right side of the holster was a small ammunition pouch. The holster was of brown leather with a flap top. The water-bottle was hung from a strap which went over the left shoulder and hung on the right side. This was an aluminium water-bottle covered in felt and with a cork stopper attached to a small chain. The water-bottle weighed about 14 oz and held 2¼ pts of liquid. The wallets worn around the neck of the horse were of leather and were strapped to the bridle. The left-hand pocket was fitted out to hold ammunition and the right to hold a pistol, which is described below.

Weapons

Sword. In 1912 officers of cavalry were equipped with a new sword modelled on the troopers' pattern of 1908. This had a steel bowl guard decorated with a honeysuckle design, but unpierced. The grip was of wood bound with fish skin and 3 silver wires to a design which made the sword come to the point more easily. It had a heavy chequered pommel, and the blade, like the troopers', was 35 in. long, 1 in. wide at the shoulder and tapered to an acute point. There were 2 scabbards, 1 covered in pigskin for wear with service dress and a steel scabbard with 2 rings for sling suspension when in full dress.

Pistol. Officers also carried the ·455 Webley service revolver. This was a heavy weapon with a cylinder of 6 chambers, and fired a cartridge with a lead ball. It was carried attached to the belt in a leather holster with a flap cover, but some of these were treated locally to remove most of the flap and leave just a strap for securing it into the holster. A small ammunition pouch was carried on the belt which would hold at the most 12 spare rounds of ammunition.

88. 5th Lancers. Trooper, 1918

Head Dress

The steel helmet was introduced in 1916 to take the place of the peaked cap. It was made of steel with a 1½-in. rim, and the dome measured 12½ in. from side to side and 14 in. from front to back. The complete diameter was 11 in. from side to side and 12 in. from front to back. The helmet was painted in khaki. The chinstrap was of elastic, covered in cloth.

Uniform

The tunic was of khaki cloth with a stand and fall collar, and it had 5 buttons down the front, of regimental pattern. Two large, flap, top pockets were worn, the flap held down by buttons. On the shoulders there was a tab held down by a brass button. On the front part of the shoulders there was a sewn-on patch. At the bottom of the tunic, on the inside of the front, was a pocket with a field dressing in it. The back of the tunic had raised seams with 2 slits at each side at the bottom. The breeches were of khaki cloth, becoming tight at the knees. The puttees were of khaki cloth and were wound from the top to the bottom.

Accoutrements

When in full marching order a pack was worn on the back, which had straps going over both shoulders and attaching to the pack again. A haversack was worn over the left shoulder and hung down on the right side. The bandolier, of brown leather with five pouches on the front to hold ammunition, was worn over the top of the haversack strap, on the left shoulder. A second bandolier and the horse gas mask were worn round the horse's neck. The soldier's gas mask was kept in a canvas bag and attached to the saddle behind the rider. There was also a signal flag hanging from the saddle. A water-bottle was hung over the right shoulder and it hung down on the left side.

Weapons

Sword. The troopers carried the sword that resulted from the discus-

sions of the last War Office Committee on Cavalry Swords. This was the pattern of 1908. It had a slender, tapered blade, 35 in. long and 1 in. wide at the shoulder, terminating in an acute point. The back was strong and the blade section was T-section. The hilt was specially designed by the Inspector of Gymnasia, so that the weapon would easily come to the point. The scabbard was of steel and was equipped with 2 rings at the mouthpiece for strapping up on the saddle.

Rifle. The rifle was designated the Short Magazine Lee Enfield. This was a breech-loading weapon of ·303 calibre, operated by a bolt action. The magazine carried 10 cartridges loaded in by chargers of 5 each that were carried in the bandoliers. The weight was 8 lb 14½ oz and the overall length was 3 ft 9½ in.

Lance. The lance pattern 1868 was also carried. This had a male bamboo staff and a forged head and butt. The head was of tricorne section and terminated in an acute point. The butt was of conical section. The weapon was equipped with red-and-white pennons at the head, and at the point of balance was a rawhide sling. It was carried in a leather bucket attached to the right stirrup iron.

89. British South Africa Police. Trooper, 1924

Head Dress

The head dress was made of cork, covered in khaki cloth, seamed with 6 partitions with an air hole at the top covered by a cloth-covered metal button. The peak measured 3 in. in the front, 2 at the sides and 4 at the back. The chinstrap was of brown leather. A 6-layer khaki pugree went round the crown of the helmet. A badge was worn on the front above the pugree. A spike was worn on top of the helmet, on ceremonial duty.

Uniform

The tunic was of green cloth with a high stand collar and pointed cuffs, and it had 6 buttons down the front. There were 2 large patch pockets, 1 on each side, the flap being held down by a regimental button. The welts and back seams were piped in the same colour cloth as the tunic, the back skirts being ornamented by double vents. The collar was ornamented with a collar badge of a lion. The shoulder tabs were of green cloth with the letters BSAP at the edge of the shoulder. The breeches were of sand-coloured bedford cord worn with brown boots.

Accoutrements

The bandolier was worn over the left shoulder with pouches on the front to hold ammunition for the rifle. The saddlecloth was in blue cloth.

Weapons

Rifle. Troopers carried the rifle, short magazine, Lee Enfield Mark I. This was a bolt-action breech-loading rifle, which fired the standard British cartridge of ·303 calibre. The total length of the rifle was 3 ft 8½ in. and its weight 8 lb 2½ oz. The magazine held 10 rounds, and was loaded by means of chargers of 5 rounds each,

which were carried in a bandolier. The weapon was fitted with a leaf sight graduated from 200 to 2,000 yd. *Lance.* For ceremonial purposes only, the lance pattern of 1868 was carried. This had a forged steel head, and the cross-section of the blade was tricorne. The butt was also forged and terminated in a blunt spike. The head of the lance was dressed with white-and-red pennons, and at the point of balance of the bamboo shaft there was a rawhide sling. The method of carriage was by inserting the butt into a leather bucket which was strapped to the right-hand stirrup iron.

90. 1st Dragoon Guards. Trumpeter, 1927

Head Dress

The helmet was of brass edged all round. The peak was pointed and had a row of laurel leaves going round the front to the side. Down the back seam ran a line of oak leaves. The plume holder was 4 in. high from the top to the crosspieces. The plume was of white horsehair for the band, being red for the troopers. The chinchain was of brass interlocking rings attached to the helmet by brass rosettes.

The helmet plate, a silver star with a Garter in the centre bearing the motto *Honi soit qui mal y pense*. In the centre of this, the figure 1 on a black background.

Uniform

Red tunic with 6 buttons down the front. The collar was of blue cloth with the regimental badge each side, edged in yellow. The cuff was of blue cloth ornamented with an Austrian knot in yellow worsted cord. The skirts were ornamented with slashes edged in yellow cord with 3 buttons on each flap. The shoulder straps were of blue cloth edged in yellow worsted lace. The aiguillettes hung from the left shoulder and were in gold cord with acorn ends. The breeches were of blue cloth with a yellow, worsted lace stripe down the outside seams.

Accoutrements

The crossbelt was in white leather and the pouch in black, with the regimental badge in the centre. The trumpet banner illustrated in the picture was the one presented to the regiment by King George V for the Delhi Durbar of 1911. It was of maroon silk with the Royal coat-of-arms on it in gold and silver lace. The usual trumpet banner was yellow silk with a black double-headed eagle on it. This was presented to the regiment by Franz Joseph, Emperor of Austria. The drum banner was of blue cloth edged all round with gold lace and fringed on 3 sides. At the centre top was the Royal coat-of-arms in gold and silver lace, under this the battle honour WATERLOO and on each side the remaining honours. Under the honour WATERLOO was the regiment's title; all the honours and the title were backed with laurel leaves.

Weapon

Sword. In 1908 cavalry troopers were issued with a new sword which had a

heavy steel guard with a beaded edge for added strength and, for the same reason, a heavy cast steel mullet around the point of entry to the tang. The grip was of Dermatine and was specially designed by Colonel Fox, Inspector of Gymnasia. The blade was 35 in. long and 1 in. wide at the shoulder and tapered regularly to a very acute point. The back was $\frac{3}{8}$ in. wide at the shoulder. The sword was carried in a tapered steel scabbard with 2 fixed rings at the mouth for suspension either from a frog or from the saddle.

91. Somaliland Camel Corps. Sergeant, 1932

Head Dress

A tied, cloth head dress, a cross between Indian and Arab, was worn by this regiment. The material was sandy-yellow coloured, and when tied, had a flap hanging down at the back of the head to the middle of the back.

Uniform

A khaki pullover of British Army pattern was worn with no collar. The badges of rank were worn on the left sleeve. A waist sash in sandy-yellow was worn, and over this a brown leather belt with bayonet and bayonet frog. The shorts were the normal issue army tropical shorts. Puttees were worn but no boots, only native sandals.

Accoutrements

A brown leather bandolier of British Cavalry pattern was worn over the right shoulder with 5 pockets for rifle ammunition.

Weapon

Rifle. Other ranks in this Corps carried the short magazine, Lee Enfield rifle Mark III, which had been introduced into service in 1907. This was the standard rifle of the British Army throughout the whole of the First World War. The overall length of the weapon was 2 ft 8½ in., and it weighed approximately 8½ lb. Although it had a maximum range of 2,800 yd, the maximum it was considered suitable for in combat was about 500 yd. It was an extremely accurate rifle and, although no longer in service with the British Army, it is still used in rifle competitions throughout the world.

92. Ayrshire Yeomanry. Officer, 1936

Head Dress

A black fur busby 6¼ in. high in the front and 7¼ in. at the back was worn; on the front, a gold gimp cockade 2 in. deep and 1½ in. wide. The bag, which fitted into the top of the busby, was of red cloth and fell down on the right-hand side to outside and centre seam, was braided in gold lace with a gold gimp button at the base. The chinchain was of gilt chain backed with red leather. The plume was of white ostrich feathers 15 in. high with a vulture plume base in red. The plume holder was a gilt corded ball with 4 leaves at the top. The caplines were of gold cord which encircled the busby 3 times, went around the body and looped up on the left side. The ends were decorated with olivets.

Uniform

The tunic was of dark blue cloth edged all round in gold gimp lace. On the front there were 6 rows of gimp cord fastening in the centre with gilt olivets. The cord across the chest ended in crowsfoot knots. On the back seams there was a double line of gimp lace forming 3 eyes at the top, passing under a gimp button and ending in an Austrian knot. The collar and cuffs were of red cloth edged in ¾-in. gold lace. The cuff was decorated with an Austrian knot. The picture shows a field officer whose collar and cuffs were highly decorated in lace. The shoulder cords were of gold chain gimp lined in blue cloth. The boots were of patent leather edged around the top in gold gimp and with gold boss on the front. Gilt spurs were worn.

Accoutrements

The web, waist, sword belt was worn under the tunic with 5 gold lace straps hanging down on the left side, 2 for the sword and 3 for the sabretache. The sabretache was of red cloth edged in gold lace with the monogram AY embroidered in the centre with a crown above and a wreath of thistles below. The pouch belt was of gold lace with silver buckle slide and tip. The pouch was of red cloth edged in lace with the same design as the sabretache on it.

Weapons

Sword. In 1912 officers of cavalry were equipped with a new sword modelled on the troopers' pattern of 1908. This had a steel bowl guard decorated with a honeysuckle design but unpierced. The grip was of wood bound with fish skin and 3 silver wires to a design which made the sword come to the point more easily. It had a heavy chequered pommel and the blade, like the troopers', was 35 in. long, 1 in. wide at the shoulder and tapered to an acute point. There were two scabbards, 1 covered in pigskin for wear with service dress and a steel scabbard with 2 rings for sling suspension when in full dress.

Note: The vignette of a Sherman tank in the background stems from the fact that in the 1930s the Ayrshire Yeomanry converted into artillery, and during the Second World War provided 2 regiments of horse artillery which served with armoured divisions in both North Africa and northern France. Troop commanders and forward observation officers were equipped with Sherman tanks so that they could go forward with the cavalry to direct the fire of their guns.

93. Governor-General's Body Guard. Trumpeter, 1938

Head Dress

A dark blue lungi was worn tied round the head and ornamented with gold stripes. The loose fringe of the lungi was stiffened and worn up like a comb above the head dress. The end was fringed and edged in gold.

Uniform

The kurta or long coat worn was scarlet double-breasted with 7 buttons each side of the plastron front. The leading edge was piped in blue. The cuffs and collar were blue, and the cuff was edged in gold lace and ornamented with an Austrian knot. The rear of the tunic had a centre vent and pleats ornamented with buttons of regimental pattern. The welts and back seams were piped in blue. A lance pattern girdle was worn around the waist, the bottom button on the tunic being flat. White breeches were worn, with black boots high at the front and cut away behind to allow easy movement of the leg. Steel spurs were worn.

Accoutrements

The trumpets were silver fanfare type with a gold-fringed banner with crown above the Star of India, surrounded by gold embroidery, 3 scrolls each side and underneath containing battle honours. A white belt with sword slings was worn under the girdle. The sword shown here was carried on the saddle. The saddle cloth was dark blue edged in 2 rows of gold lace with a blue light between. The saddle cover was white lambskin edged in dark blue cloth vandyked.

Note: The horses of the trumpeters were white.

Weapon

Sword. The sword carried was the Indian Army version of the 1908 pattern trooper's sword. This had the same blade, 35 in. long with a strong back tapering to an acute point, but the guard in sheet steel with a beaded edge and heavy steel mullet around the point of entry in the tang, was slightly smaller to accommodate the shorter grip. This grip was in polished wood, and although modelled on Colonel Fox's pattern, having a recess for the thumb, the grip itself was slighter and designed for the smaller hand of the Indian. It was carried in a steel scabbard with 2 rings at the mouthpiece for carriage, strapped up on the saddle or belt.

94. 13th (Duke of Cornwall's Own) Lancers. Drummer, 1938

Head Dress

The lungi was of blue cloth with gold and light blue stripes of regimental pattern.

Uniform

The loose frock coat or kurta as it was known was of dark blue cloth with red stand collar and usual lancer-style pointed cuffs, both edged in gold lace. The kurta had an opening to the waist in front. The leading edge and all the seams and welts were in red. The kurta had 4 front buttons, the bottom one being flat to go under the cummerbund, which was in red patterned cloth of Kashmir pattern. The epaulettes were of linked chain, and lancer aiguillettes were worn around the neck and looped up on the left breast.

The breeches were of white cloth worn with leather knee protectors to prevent injury to the drummer from the drums. Worn with the breeches were dark blue puttees of regimental pattern with black boots and spurs.

Accoutrements

The waist-belt was of brown leather with regimental-pattern buckle. The shabraque had a plain front, the rear being affixed under the leopard-skin seat cloth (with leopard head to rear). This was of blue cloth edged in silver lace with a train of red cloth. The tips of the tails had silver and red tassels, the tail being heavily embroidered in both gold and silver lace. The whole device was a crown in the top angle of 2 crossed lances, with pennons. In the centre of the lances the number 13, the 1 and 3 in the 2 side angles. Crossing the base angle was a scroll bearing the regimental title. Under this device was a wreath with a cipher in the centre and crown above. The drum banner was square, of dark blue cloth edged in silver lace, with a red train. The bottom edge had a silver fringe. The device was much more elaborate than the shabraque. The crossed lances and crown with the number 13 appeared in the centre, with a scroll above bearing the honour GUZNEE. Around this, a wreath of laurel leaves with battle honours entwined within the leaves and branches. The throat plume was red.

95. Transjordan Frontier Force. Sergeant, 1938

Head Dress

The head dress worn by all ranks of the Transjordan Frontier Force was a black astrakhan kalpack. A fly on the right in scarlet, and extending over the crown, was worn. This was embroidered with criss-cross gold lace patterning. On the front of the head dress in white metal was worn the badge of the force, a crown surmounted in circular scroll and in the centre a winged eagle.

Uniform

A khaki drill or India-type tunic, buttoning to the waist but open to middle thigh, was worn. The tunic had a stand cover, closed at the neck, and 2 patch pockets on each breast. Both cuffs were pointed and of same colour. A scarlet waist sash was worn tying up on the left hip and hanging down, ending in panels. Chain mail epaulettes were worn on both shoulders. Bedford cord riding breeches were worn and dark blue puttees wound from below the knee to the ankle. Brown boots and steel spurs with brown leather straps were worn.

Accoutrements

A 5-pocket bandolier in brown leather of British Cavalry pattern was worn over the left shoulder and a brown, leather, cavalry pattern waistbelt with a small pouch on the right front, was worn. Two short sword slings hung on the left side. A rifle bucket was carried on the horse.

Weapons

Sword. The sword carried by troopers of this force was the 1908 pattern, which had been approved on 2 July of that year. This had a narrow, single-edged blade 35 in. long, 1 in. wide at the shoulder and with a regular taper to a spear point. It had an extremely strong back and was fullered from 1 in. below the shoulder to within 9 in. of the point. It was carried in a tapered steel scabbard with no shoe and two fixed rings on opposite sides just below the mouthpiece so that it could be worn either on short slings from the belt or could be strapped up on the cantle of the saddle.

Rifle. Also carried in a saddle bucket was a ·303 short magazine Lee Enfield rifle.

96. Life Guards. Trooper, 1953

Head Dress

A white metal helmet was worn not only by the troopers but also by farriers of the Life Guards and the Royal Horse Guards. The helmet was of the same basic pattern as that worn by Dragoon Regiments (except the 2nd), and had a pointed peak edged all around with brass trim, the back peak also being trimmed in the same way. Across the helmet above the peak was brass ornamentation, laurel on the left and oak-leaves on the right. A broad strap of oak-leaf-patterned brass ran down the back seam from the top to the brass trimming. The badge was a large oval with white metal Garter star in the centre, the oval being encircled with the collar of the Order of the Garter and with a St. George badge hanging from the centre. The whole badge was surrounded by a wreath of oak and laurel leaves and surmounted by the crown of the reigning monarch. The top of the helmet had a rayed plate in which was fitted the plume holder, a white metal stem in a brass ball. The plume was white. The chinchains were of brass interlocking chain, backed with leather and attached to the helmet on each side with brass rosettes.

Uniform

The tunic was of scarlet cloth with blue collar and cuffs, the blue collar edged all round with gold lace of regimental pattern. The cuffs were gauntlet cuffs in blue cloth with a 'V' in gold lace with a regimental button at the apex. The leading and bottom edges were in blue. The back of the skirts had 2 slashed flaps, each flap having 3 buttons of regimental pattern. The epaulettes were in blue cloth edged in gold lace. The breast plates were of white metal, the 2 halves held together by brass shoulder straps at the top and a white buff strap at the waist. The back and front plates were ornamented with brass studs round the edge. The breeches were of white buff leather. The boots were thigh length with large pointed wings on the outside edge.

Accoutrements

The crossbelt was of white buff leather with a red flask cord. The pouch was of black leather with a brass coat-of-arms in the centre ornamented with honour scrolls. The gauntlets were of white leather. The horse cloth was of white lambskin edged in blue vandyked cloth.

Weapon

Sword. Troopers carried the 1892 pattern sword with a sheet steel hand guard, pierced and decorated with scrolls, in which were included the letters HC, surmounted by a crown. The backpiece was plain and the grip of fish skin bound with 3 silver wires. The blade measured around the slight curve $34\frac{1}{2}$ in. from shoulder to point and was $1\frac{1}{4}$ in. wide at the shoulder. It was carried in a heavy steel scabbard with a cast iron shoe and 2 rings for sling suspension.

INDEX